THE NATIONAL LOVE, SEX & MARRIAGE TEST

The National Love, Sex & Marriage Test

by Rubin Carson

Are You As Good a Mate As You Think You Are?

BASED ON THE NBC-TV "BIG EVENT"

(A WARREN V. BUSH PRODUCTION)

A Dolphin Book

DOUBLEDAY & COMPANY, INC.

GARDEN CITY, NEW YORK

1978

Dolphin Books
DOUBLEDAY & COMPANY, INC.
ISBN: 0-385-14298-6
Library of Congress Catalog Card Number 77–18625
Copyright © 1978 by WARREN V. BUSH PRODUCTIONS, INC.

First Edition

contents

preface

BY C. RAY FOWLER, PH.D.

Executive Director,
American Association of
Marriage and Family Counselors

In American society, marriage is not as inevitable as death, but it is more inevitable than taxes. That is, marriage happens to nearly everyone in our society. Of every ten Americans, nine and a half will get married as adults. Of course, many will marry before they are adults; and, for many more who marry over the age of eighteen, the decision will not be a very adult one. That is largely because, in our society, many of our expectations about marriage are unadulterated romantic nonsense! My reason for believing that marriage has now passed taxes as an "inevitable" is very simple Everyone tries to avoid taxes and at least a few must be successful at it, whereas no one these days seems to try to avoid marriage. On the contrary, everyone seems to pursue marriage, some again, again, and again.

This book is about marriage. It is also about love and sex. So it has something for everyone. It is not a how-to book complete with anatomical assignments. Nor is it a solemn homily on the subject. Rather, it is a delightfully painless blending of scholarly common sense, real-life interviews, and positive good humor directed at ourselves.

Human behavioral scientists have developed a great deal of important and accurate information about human personality and interaction, especially as it relates to love, sex, and marriage. This book incorporates insights from some of the leading authorities as well as information from reliable research. The author has paid careful attention to the scientific sources of information available to him. He has achieved a balanced presentation of information and anecdote which will help the average reader to face the important question "Are you as good a mate as you think you are?" This is not a heavy excavation into the archaeology of your personal psyche. Nor is it a dull lecture on the theory of mate selection.

We can assure you that you will be informed, but not with the "last word." The last word on love, sex, and marriage will not be spoken so long as at least two human beings continue to exist on this planet of ours! And, finally, we are sure that you will enjoy the experience of participating in THE NATIONAL LOVE, SEX & MARRIAGE TEST!

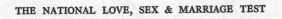
THE NATIONAL LOVE, SEX & MARRIAGE TEST

introduction

The creators of THE NATIONAL LOVE, SEX & MARRIAGE TEST dedicate this book and test . . .

. . . to the new breed of Romantics who, because of our highly transient age, longer life expectancy, and changing sexual values, realize that the vow "'til death do us part" usually means about 8.7 years (depending upon which partner registered the china pattern at the onset);

. . . to the realists, who believe that a committed, sexually exclusive relationship is still the safest place in town to be;

. . . to people of taste from both camps, who have always believed that finding and living with their Romantic Ideal might be accomplished with less phoniness and greater authority, style, and above all good humor.

With these formalities behind us, let us turn to the book itself. Our book is not like any other work on how to make a better marriage, because it speaks in many voices. In order of appearance: the voices are the producers of the NBC "Big Event" special on which this book is based; a veritable chorus of the leading experts in the field of relationships who were interviewed; and, lastly, the people from the University of Southern California who created the test itself.

Aside from presenting a general overview of "where relationships are at" today, this book is unique in that it is a highly opinionated, sometimes quirky, relationship guide geared to the special needs of, for lack of any other appellation, the dyed-in-the-wool Romantic or the Expectation Buff.

The category of Expectation Buff includes almost all of us: that red-blooded, typical American type who holds firmly to the most widely held and most pernicious family myth of all—*the quest for the perfect relationship.*

Let's face it. The incessant search for "more" is a direct descendant of American optimism and, above all, Romanticism. The issues our book deals with parallel those things a true Buff looks for in marriage. In order of appearance:

1. That marriage will provide you with constant romance.

2. That a good relationship should be smooth as silk.

3. That sex will be limitless in an ongoing relationship.

4. That instant communication comes with the territory.

5. That changing sex roles will put marriage on self-destruct.

6. That marriage provides you with built-in emotional security.

One of the primary goals of the creators of THE NATIONAL LOVE, SEX & MARRIAGE TEST is to let you find out "what kind of mate you really are." It is only through this process that you can truly learn to take care of yourself and, at the same time, be responsive to (and thus able to take care of) another person.

Enough of how we got that way. On to our journey and how to use this test.

The opening chapter will familiarize you with marital myths and expectations so that you can become accustomed to looking at the whole confusing arena of marriage from a new perspective and hopefully gain some new awareness.

Each of the following chapters deals with the most pervasive, tenacious American marital myths (we could have had at least sixty), followed by commentaries from our chorus of experts. Each chapter then concludes with a test on the issues discussed (herein and forever after to be known as THE NATIONAL LOVE, SEX & MARRIAGE TEST), especially created in collaboration with noted marriage counselor Professor Thomas Lasswell, former chairman of the Department of Sociology at the University of Southern California, and Professor Eleen A. Bauman, expert on marriage and the family at California State University, Los Angeles.

The tests will challenge you with questions pertaining to these six dynamic areas in contemporary relationships:

1. LOVE. How well do you understand what a loving relationship between two people might be?

2. FIGHTING. How fair do you fight and how skilled are you at solving difficulties in your own relationship?

3. SEX. How open are you about your own sexuality? How likely are you to have a satisfying sexual relationship?

4. FEELINGS. How realistically do you deal with your feelings? How sensitive are you to your mate's feelings?

5. ROLES. How much do you depend on role expectations to guide your relationship?

6. TRUST. How important is it to control your mate's life? How much freedom do you have in your own relationship?

A brief warning: Your score on the test does not determine whether you are good or bad as a mate. It merely measure just how realistic you, fellow Expectation Buff, are about expectations in such areas as LOVE, FIGHT-ING, SEX, FEELINGS, ROLES, and TRUST.

In Chapter 8 you get a bonus: a special sex test to be taken by yourself and/or hopefully your partner. This test was created by Carly Buchanan, Ph.D., specialist in sex education, and sexual therapists Eleanor Katzman, M.A., M.F.C., and Sam Katzman, M.A., M.S., and will enable you to amalgamate all the things we have studied and put them to some immediate (and fun) use.

And, finally, a polling and public sampling is presented in Chapter 9 so you can check your scores with those of over a thousand other Americans who have taken this test. The sampling was conducted by Professor Eleen A. Bauman, one of the codevelopers of our test, and Professor Richard G. Mitchell, Jr., at California State University at Los Angeles, in conjunction with Facts Consolidated of Los Angeles, California.

Now is the time for a final, brief rededication. We, the creators of THE NATIONAL LOVE, SEX & MARRIAGE TEST, dedicate our journey to people everywhere who want to celebrate sexually exclusive, committed relationships, and more especially to our fellow Romantics, who believe that the Romantic dream is the most real thing they possess, who are convinced that marriage is the best setting for making it come alive, and who believe that the American Home (in spite of Brave New Marriage advocates) is not only the safest but the most exciting place in town.

great expectations

Welcome, gentle voyager. Shall we begin?

The year is 2001. A man and a woman are dining out to celebrate their engagement. Calmly and analytically, they discuss their future together. The marriage contract will be a standard three-year one, renewable in 2004 if both partners are still satisfied. Sloppy concepts like "love," "communication," and "intimacy" don't enter the picture. Except for a few die-hard romantics, people stopped worrying about such things in the 1980s and, besides, this couple scored 98, an almost perfect computer match.

Children will be out of the question, since the screening process and parent-training courses are too time-consuming. Our about-to-be-weds decide to pencil in sterilization appointments for the following week. The future settled, they split the tab and leave.

The above is a model—perhaps a panacea—for American marriage, according to many future-oriented sociologists. They advocate that, to end divorce right this very minute, marriage should be computerized into a rational process (and couples should not have to wait for 2001!). They should choose marriage partners as they do orthopedic mattresses—selecting the one that is best tailored to their needs.

Besides the three- and five-year marriage contracts, there should be permanent childless marriages for the more unfettered types, plus all sorts of unisex marriages and group setups with a variety of unusual but intriguing variations.

So much for the futurists. We, the producers of THE NATIONAL LOVE, SEX & MARRIAGE TEST, can only applaud their efforts to make our much-battered institution of marriage more predictable, malleable, and less of a life shock to the participants.

Those of us left to cope with marriage-of-the-present are not so fortunate. Inflamed by passion, giddy with excitement, torn by the desire to please each other and to put the best foot forward, all the couples embarking on marriage or live-in relationships, 1970s style, have is each other and perhaps a dog-eared copy of *The Joy of Sex* . . . and, of course, the problem to which our journey throughout the United States and our test addresses itself.

The problem is that we enter any deeply committed relationship burdened by fantasies, dreams, expectations, wishes, mirages, inflated notions, and utopian visions of what another person is supposed to do for us.

We enter a relationship hoping that it will be a kind of cornucopia whence all blessings flow, a kind of free clinic, a refuge where all the slings and arrows that the world hurls at us will be deflected.

To sum it up simply, the typical American brings dozens of *Expectations* into a relationship. We are victimized not only by the demands of a close, intimate relationship between a man and a woman but by our sincerely held expectations about what those demands might be. And when the expectations are brutally dashed on the shores of reality, relationships start to crumble.

When this romantic, overidealized vision finally does crumble, each blames the other for failing to pass an exam he never knew he was taking. As we went around the country interviewing experts in counseling, psychiatry, and allied fields, most experts said that the first, most vital thing the Expectation Buff must learn is to *stop blaming the mate for the problem.*

This is difficult. After all, if you're a disappointed Expectation Buff, out of simple self-preservation you advance the concept that you, the Buff, are a reasonable, put-upon embodiment of virtue, perhaps with a *few* bad habits of your own (like smoking too much or yelling at the cat too loud). Your mate, on the other hand, is childish, moody, hysterical, extravagant, and *all or more of these.* The distressing alternative, which the experts hold is the most difficult for people to learn, is *you must accept responsibility for yourself!*

We asked Linda Carson, M.A., M.F.C., and therapist, to sum up this whole area of expectations:

"Happily ever after" may be one of the most misleading and therefore destructive expressions in our literature. Most of us were raised on stories which left us with the impression that married life was an endlessly blissful experience, and these fairy tales were the basis of many of our expectations for marriage. Hollywood did its share, too, supplying our all-too-willing minds with romantic images of true lovers standing joyfully at the altar . . . fade out . . . The End. We left the theaters contentedly assuming that marriage was a continuation of this lovely scene.

In retrospect it is easy enough to see that these impressions were inadequate, to say the least. How, then, can we explain their continued popularity over so many generations, despite the fact that people *must* have discovered the false representation of reality which these myths offer? We can't really blame the books or the movies alone, since it is only the public (meaning us) who decides their success. Let's face it: Reality is difficult—if it's not pretty, we would prefer not to look at it. We choose, therefore, to maintain our lovely fantasies, even at the price of fooling ourselves.

Thank you, friend therapist. Now, on to our fantasies.

2

EXPECTATION #1:

that marriage will provide you with constant romance

(This also goes for couples
who are only "living-in.")

My personal definition of love is never very satisfying to anybody else. I've done research on the process
by which children come to define love as they're growing up and it turns out that if you ask, say, third-
graders if they've ever been in love, about half of
them will say that they have. And, if you ask fifth-
graders, about half. And seventh-graders. And on up,
all the way through high school, about half of them
will say they've been in love. Now, if you ask each of
these people when they were *first* in love, it turns out
that the modal time they were first in love was within
the last year. That's just not sensible. If you ask them
when they had their first *date*, it's a pyramid—a few
people in the sixth grade, more people in the ninth
grade, more people in the tenth grade. If you ask them
how many had a *kiss*, you find a pyramid. But if you
ask them how many were in love, you find a very
straight thing. And we finally decided that what that
meant was that, every year, they redefined what love
was. So if you ask a seventh-grader who said he was
in love for the first time this year, "Well, what about

last year when I interviewed you—you said you were in love, then, too?" he says, with embarrassment, "Oh, *that!* Well, that was just infatuation. What did I know about love then? Until I met Mary Ann, I didn't know what love was." So I believe, and you can demonstrate, that people redefine love on each occasion and therefore, I believe that the only defensible definition of love is that emotion which you feel for your *current* involvement.

Carlfred B. Broderick, Ph.D.
Los Angeles, California

The reader is now aware that most of us Americans enter the marital or "living-in" state burdened by deeply ingrained expectations. We usually embark upon a committed union, not for what we can bring to it, but because we have some fantasy-filled notions of the rewards *it* will bring to *us*.

The typical searchers (i.e., Expectation Buffs) look for a marriage that is harmonious, loving, and chock full of communication, understanding, shared feelings, self-disclosure, mutual respect, sexual excitement, daily joy, and, in some cases, fulfillment through children.

However, when *all* of these fail to materialize as they expected them to, these disappointed pilgrims join the ranks of our million per year statistics.

Now, mind you, these millions of people are not anti-marriage, but they *are* anti-*their*-marriage. Thus, according to U. S. Census Bureau predictions, 30 per cent of divorced persons will "try again." And many will try a second and even a third time, frenetically looking for what could be called Hollywood's "Made-in-Utopia Marriage."

They go through high school dating at forty, fifty, and older, live together, break up, try again—always on the relentless search for that "happily-ever-after" state which keeps eluding them.

The melancholy fact remains: When you ask an Expectation Buff why he embarks on his first, second, or third marriage, he invariably answers: "It was love," "That romantic bit," or "Cupid made me."

So before we test the powers of your own romantic notions, let us plunge into our first Expectation: that marriage will continue to provide us with constant romance.

We all know, having been there ourselves, that American teen-agers are programmed to believe that marriage (or living together) will provide them with a constant source of Romantic Feelings, the general euphoria that provides the sentimental movies like *Love Story* and *The Way We Were* or the way we *thought* we were.

Wouldn't you think that the marriage experts that we interviewed, being so realistic, grounded, and credentialed, would dismiss this expectation out of hand? Not so, much to our surprise. Most experts we interviewed believed that a certain amount of idealistic romance is essential.

But, is it possible? Our experts say that for short, regular periods, *yes*. Having accepted this premise, then, the next thing we must face is how do you create this kind of love?

Well, you can't buy closeness and intimacy, regardless of how many trips to Europe, new sofas for the living room, or mink coats are operative. The relationship is given the chance to achieve what we, of THE NATIONAL LOVE, SEX & MARRIAGE TEST, humbly submit for your consideration as a revised version of Romantic Love: *The Realistic Romantic Ideal.*

By Romantic Ideal, we mean sharing your sexual self and your emotional self with someone whom you are willing to invest everything in. That one person whose qualities seem to fall into those areas that are the most valued to you. Namely, a person who reminds you very much of yourself or, put another way, the self you had always hoped (but never really believed) you might become. In short, a person who completes you.

Now, how do you know if a person is your bona fide Romantic Ideal? Wouldn't that be more like infatuation? Okay, we said it, and we're glad. All Realistic Romantic Love starts with what is commonly known as infatuation. And thank heaven for it.

Infatuation, or passion, draws people together so that Realistic Love can happen. Now, let's take a moment to arrive at a working definition of Love.

According to the vast majority of experts we questioned, they seemed to favor Harry Stack Sullivan's version: (True) Love can be defined as caring about the other person's life traumas *at least* as much as your own.

Once you've resolved the problems created in large part by the unrealistic expectations of a typical myth-proliferated relationship, you relate to this person *in* marriage essentially the same way you did *before* marriage. Like two separate individuals and, of course, like lovers.

Now, courtship, as we all know, includes well-intentioned (yet deceptive) fan dancing, as well as all other forms of day and night false advertising. After marriage, the Styrofoam curtain drops and people experience each other with curlers in their hair, mixed but never matched checking accounts, etc., etc.

The experts' feeling is that prenuptial game-playing has to do with cultural expectations. Americans *expect* to be euphoric before marriage, when everybody is putting his best foot forward. Each presents the other with the behavior he or she desires, resulting in a better picture of themselves than they have ever had before.

So the old cultural imperative goes—everyone discovers the real person *after* the ceremony is over and the wedding offerings are safely tucked into the cedar hope chest. It's then that the real person emerges. After the kids, the rent, and the mulching bills—presumably this is what marriage is all about—you live the rest of your life with the Real Person: Someone you rarely send Candy-Grams to or, in many cases, even say "Please" and "Thank you" to.

We are all victims of a self-destroying prophecy: Romance tends to die after monogamous marriage.

It is a small wonder that our first marital expectation of Constant Romance is such an albatross around our combined necks. On one hand, we are raised to believe that marriage incorporates Romantic Love and, on the other hand, our heads and the yearly divorce statistics from the

Bureau of Census tell us it won't. It is a Gordian knot, a total muck-up if there ever was one.

Without Romantic Love as a deep connection in the marriage, disappointed couples are perpetually residing at some Court of the Doges, with nonstop betrayal and broken dreams and disappointment behind every nook and cafe curtain. Both mates know that the other would like some of the spontaneous tokens of esteem and caring they presented to each other during courtship, only the "other" is too uncaring to figure this out for him or her self.

After all, weren't they both responsible for making the other feel adored? And, what is more, neither is going to come right out and ask for it, in spite of the fact that he or she yearns for it desperately.

An Expectation Buff feels too humiliated and vulnerable to come right out and ask for *anything* that is standard equipment on any deeply held marital expectation. Besides, didn't the other know how to please you *without your asking* during the courtship period? Of course!

Now, back to our prototype of a marriage that encompasses a Realistic Romantic Ideal. Our prototype: a relationship where you could not tell the difference between the courtship and postcourtship periods. Our own Brave New Marriage where each person reflects the other's vision of himself, in almost the same way before the wedding vows were exchanged. Our device for creating this relationship we will call Ideal Feedback.

Here is the recipe. You can be sure that most people have a somewhat negative picture of themselves, but, at the same time, have a nagging Walter Mittyish dream about the great person they *really* are. When someone comes along and recognizes that you are, indeed, this lovable person and keeps reminding you of it, it is one of human existence's great experiences. In addressing this, our first marital expectation, a truly Romantic Marriage is one in which you are constantly an "ideal" picture of yourself. Only *more* so.

In a marriage of two loving grownups, after a lot of hard work and lots of bumps, you are getting and giving this Ideal Feedback all the time. You grow from receiving it, but, most of all, you grow from giving it. When each partner keeps getting this validation of his worth in sexual, emotional, and intellectual terms from someone *he* respects, each begins to feel quite a worthwhile person.

Through some not-altogether mysterious process, you become this person. The more you make another person feel this way, the more you grow yourself.

And now, for a few words from our loyal friends—the therapists who have more experience in treating individuals than couples. Shouldn't the way you feel about yourself determine who you really are? they say.

If you depend upon this Ideal Feedback, aren't you giving a kind of "life and death" power to another person? What if things change and that person stops loving you, for example? Well, it's certainly a fair question. Especially in view of the success of so many books like *How to Be Your Own Best Friend,* the authors of which will be interviewed throughout this book.

In a relationship that has the kind of caring we propose, there is not much possibility of a person running out of his "supply" of love. In addition, there will be a minimum of infidelity, boredom, hopelessness, feelings of invisibility, or any of the other syndromes that afflict contemporary relationships and provide psychiatrists with large case loads.

Each shared experience becomes such a unifying, pleasurable event that the only thing you think about is that here, surrounded by an often-dangerous world, you have a miraculous vehicle for acquiring pleasure. When two people try to achieve this, and really work at it, it's like a continuous, ongoing spiral—a spiral of growth.

In the opinion of THE NATIONAL LOVE, SEX & MARRIAGE TEST, that is the reason noncommitted relationships are ultimately self-defeating. If a relationship has any deep romantic connection at all, you wish it to be permanent. You wish it to continue in this ongoing spiral of pleasure. It's a lack of this component that lends destructiveness to many of the Brave New Marriage styles, in spite of their admitted romantic potential.

As practicing Expectation Buffs and normal, insecure bipeds, we don't think you can start caring for yourself unless someone helps you. We are all dependent upon others. Unless someone else gives you some vision of what you might become, it's pretty hard to acquire it on your own. We all need, for lack of any other name, inspiration.

The favorite song of THE NATIONAL LOVE, SEX & MARRIAGE TEST is "You Are Almost Nobody 'Til Somebody Loves You." There! We said it, and we're glad. Now it's time for the experts to have their say on this topic.

What Part Does Romance Really *Play
in Marriage?*

I will quote myself and, as I have said for many
years to my clients, especially my marriage and family
clients, "You had better not marry anybody you don't
love, but you had also better not marry everybody you
do love."

Romantic love, and especially what H. G. Wells
once called "loving kindness," is an essential part of a
good marriage. Now, the romantic part doesn't last
terribly long, but it sparks a marriage, it aids it, and
the loving kindness allows marriage to go on with all
of its foremost inevitable hassles and troubles.

Dr. Albert Ellis
New York, New York

More marriages get into trouble, I suppose, from
the woman's point of view because suddenly she feels
that attention is lacking to her, that the man does not
seem enchanted with her, fascinated with her, that he
doesn't pay her compliments any more, that he doesn't
buy her clothes, that he no longer shows fascination
with her as a woman. He may still be having sex with
her regularly but she may feel that this is sort of a
perfunctory thing that he is doing. Men, on the other
hand, have difficulty understanding this in a woman
because men, perhaps, are not as oriented around their
own physical desirability. I think a man, once he gets
out of early adolescence, begins to understand that it's
kind of what he has achieved, the kind of success that
he is, whether he is regarded as an intelligent person—

these are the criteria of his desirability. So, he doesn't really expect his wife to make a big fuss over his physical appearance—to tell him he looks handsome, to tell him he looks nice. This is almost a feminine criterion. Some men don't particularly care about this. You never hear a husband bitterly accusing his wife, "You never tell me I look handsome any more," "You never tell me you like the way I look," but you certainly hear it from wives once they get to ventilating and some of this frustration comes out.

Even a relationship that is good cannot *constantly* be good. Every marriage, every relationship has its doldrums, it has its bad days. Things don't really keep coasting on a nice, even level. And yet people will somehow tend to look at the bad days and remember them and say, "Oh, my God, what happened to us—it's been a week since we really even talked to one another." And, okay, that doesn't mean there is something disastrously wrong. It's good you picked it up. But I don't think anybody really has a perfect relationship and, somehow, this is the expectation—that if you set up everything right, if you don't rock the boat too much, things are just going to go swimmingly. They don't. It doesn't happen.

Anthony Pietropinto, M.D.
New York, New York

Well, I think it's a necessary part of marriage, like it's necessary to have hope about going into something, and like it's necessary to have some of the light touches in marriage. I think a deep romance is necessary but, like everything else, it's not the whole thing. It's part of the context.

When I think of romance, I think of great love stories, first of all, and behind that is the feeling that I could matter enough to another person and that person could matter enough to me so that when things are tough we could somehow fall back on this romantic connection, and that there would be light, and beauty, and humor, and attentiveness. I think all of these are part of romance.

Dr. Virginia Satir
San Francisco, California

When marriage is good, you give up a lot of excess baggage—you give up romantic notions, the romantic notion that "I'm going to be swept off my feet and irresistibly drawn into an ecstacy of some sort without my having to lift a finger for it, and that we will live happily ever after without having to bring creativity and thoughtfulness to the process." That's what has to be given up. That, in my view, is the biggest obstacle to a good marriage.

Bernard Berkowitz
New York, New York

Romance has a two-edged impact on marriage. For one thing, it's the cheap motivator toward marriage. I have been impressed by the fact that almost no couple will admit they married without loving each other; or they may say (when trying to get out of marriage), "Well, maybe I never loved you," or (when trying to hurt each other), "I never loved you." So, in our culture, it's the most important and most legitimate reason to get married and the most important excuse that people use for getting out of marriage. To get married without love is considered a tragic and unwise thing.

But the other edge of the sword is that romance, by its very nature, consists of a series of expectations which may or may not be fulfilled and are likely to be disappointed and, therefore, it has the second quality of being one of the occasions of dissatisfaction and disillusionment. In that regard, studies show that men more than women are romantics. Women are more pragmatic, their expectations more realistic. Men are the ones who expect their wives to be rather extraordinary and superhuman.

> Carlfred B. Broderick, Ph.D.
> Los Angeles, California

I think we're brought up to be romantic—by literature to a certain extent, and things in the media emphasize romance, TV, and the Gothic novel. Somebody told me the other day that greeting card companies are selling more and more romantic greeting cards and more and more flowers are being sold. Something's happening with people, I suspect, in terms of wanting to return to some of what they think were the kinds of things that held marriages together years ago. I don't think romance is one of those, but somehow we still seem to be a very romantic nation and think that we have to be in love before we marry.

> Marcia Lasswell, Ph.D.
> Pomona, California

To me, romance would be dinner in candlelight with a glass of wine . . . or it could be something quite different, with nothing happening, and still be a very intense relationship.

> Dr. Mary Calderone
> Old Brookville, New York

Romantic love is an integral part of marriage. I think for married people who are finding it kind of dull, I think checking into a motel would be sort of fun. Or some crazy surprise, some inexpensive gift, something funny.

Ann Landers
Chicago, Illinois

What Has Surprised You Most About Your Marriage?

The biggest surprise was that the marriage, and sex itself, kept getting better and better. I'd heard so much about how it's great and then it goes downhill from there. It doesn't. It keeps getting better and better. That's incredible. I've been so pleased to be able to help people to achieve that same kind of result in their own marriage. But I found myself quite surprised when it happened to me.

Bernard Berkowitz
New York, New York

It was what it is: being loved every single day, every single hour, all the time. It's wonderful.

Mildred Newman
New York, New York

Well, about my ex-marriage, the biggest surprise was, I suppose that we had a lot of time to ourselves. We thought that because we had a lot of time to ourselves and we worked very hard, we would be able to get along. But then when my ex-wife, who was a dancer, broke her leg and wasn't able to devote that much time to her work, we seemed to have too much time together, and that didn't work.

Dr. Albert Ellis
New York, New York

That I was married to a person who had a whole different view of the world than I did. My husband is a physician, and he believes that almost everything goes on in the body, and I believe that most of the problems are in the mind. And we've been fighting eyeball to eyeball for twenty-eight years.

Dr. Joyce Brothers
Fort Lee, New Jersey

Well, I married a man almost as complicated as I am. I think it's almost impossible to answer that because he is so different all the time.

Dr. Mary Calderone
Old Brookville, New York

The biggest surprise was that it ended, because it was a wonderful marriage for thirty-six years.

Ann Landers
Chicago, Illinois

Well, the shock is that, after twenty years, I still look forward to him coming home. I really enjoy seeing him. I like to listen to his ideas. I really find him wonderful company.

Jane Appleton
Cambridge, Massachusetts

I don't think I had any really big surprises, because we knew each other very well before we got married, several years.

Dr. Theodore Isaac Rubin
New York, New York

My biggest surprise was that my wife was as open and as congruent as she is. The reason it was a surprise to me was because I wasn't. I was more anxious and more vulnerable than she was. She gave me a lot of confidence in myself as a person.

Dr. Michael Carrera
New York, New York

I remember the first morning I was married, my husband was up bright and early whistling in the shower. I'm a night person, and I remember thinking, "What have I done?"

Marcia Lasswell, Ph.D.
Pomona, California

I think the first thing that surprised me was that there were so many parts of the person I married that I didn't know. These weren't necessarily bad parts, but they were just parts I didn't know. I got a jog thinking that I knew somebody when I didn't really know them. For instance, he was much more interested in things like cooking and things in the kitchen than I'd ever known he had any aptitude for or interest in. Now that was interesting. That turned out to be a really good thing for me. But at first it felt like an invasion, because I'm good at those things, too.

Dr. Virginia Satir
San Francisco, California

PART 1 OF THE TEST:
"LOVE"

TEST INSTRUCTIONS

Before you take the first section of the test, a brief word on how to proceed.

In each section, circle the letter of the answer you think is the most correct. Following the questions in each section of the test, the correct answers are listed with explanations. Check your answers against the experts and give yourself *10 points* for each one you've answered correctly. Then add up your score for each section . . . and don't forget to record it in the blank provided.

At the end of the scoring and evaluation for the test on TRUST (Chapter 7), you will find a form for entering your scores from each of the test sections to determine your total score . . . and a breakdown so you can see how well you did in comparison with our national sampling . . . on THE NATIONAL LOVE, SEX & MARRIAGE TEST.

Ready . . . set . . . GO!

In 1974 a Roper poll found that, for the majority of Americans (83 per cent of the women and 77 per cent of the men), love was the primary reason for marrying.

The capacity for love is inherent in human beings. We are basically social creatures who fare very poorly in isolation. For all the interest and debate love has generated over the centuries, it is still a difficult idea to define or explain. When a strong emotional attraction for another person is felt, this attraction is often labeled "love."

This first section of the test will measure your understanding of the place of *LOVE* in an intimate relationship.

Questions on "Love"

QUESTIONS:

Circle T for those statements you think are true and F for those you think are false.

1. Jealousy is natural if you really love your mate. (T) F

2. True love is something that always lasts a lifetime. T (F)

3. Taking my side—no matter what—shows my partner loves me. T (F)

4. Just because two people break up doesn't mean they never loved each other. (T) F

5. If people really love each other, they don't have to say it. (T) F

SCORING:

For each correct answer, give yourself *10 points*.

MY SCORE FOR "LOVE" _____

Please turn the page for the correct answers.

Answers for
Part 1 of the Test: "Love"

---

1. *"Jealousy is natural if you really love your mate."*
   FALSE

   Jealousy is only natural for some persons' concepts of love. Many people do not include jealousy in their definitions of love at all and many consider it to be destructive to love. For those persons for whom jealousy does occur, *how they behave* in response to jealous *feelings* is more important for their relationship than whether they feel jealous.

2. *"True love is something that always lasts a lifetime."*
   FALSE

   "True love" clearly takes different forms at different points in the family life cycle. For example, the true love of a childless couple may involve very different feelings from the true love of the parents of a small child. A widow who truly loved her first husband may truly love her second—or third.

3. *"Taking my side—no matter what—shows my partner loves me."*
   FALSE

   Taking a person's "side" can be destructive if the result is not good for that person, or if the action is taken merely to avoid a fight. Some partners function very effectively as "sounding boards" for their mates. Others submit to power plays to the detriment of both (the wife of the alcoholic who gives her husband a bottle for Christmas, or the husband of the obese woman who brings her a box of candy). Respecting differences leads to a more fulfilling relationship.

4. *"Just because two people break up doesn't mean they never loved each other."*

TRUE

People are not always able to live comfortably with those they love. This is easily seen with family members (e.g., mother and child who lived together very happily at one point but not at another). Every person is different—every love affair is different. People change. To stop changing means to stop living.

5. *"If people really love each other, they don't have to say it."*

FALSE

People who love each other will find a way to make their love known, whether they say it or not. Saying "I love you," however, reinforces the belief of many people that they are, indeed, loved. The basis for any relationship is communication, which is the cement between two people.

SCORING:

Give yourself 10 points if you answered "True" on question 4, and ten points for each response of "False" on questions 1, 2, 3, and 5.

EVALUATION:

The higher your score, the better you understand what a loving relationship between two people can be.

3

EXPECTATION #2:

*that a good relationship
should be smooth as silk*

I know one couple who save everything for a whole
week. They either write down or keep in their minds
all of their arguments and they go out to dinner once
a week and go over all their irritations and angers that
have been built up for the whole week. Being out in
public keeps them from beating up on each other. The
restaurant itself, I imagine, has to be very fancy so
that you can't shout too much.

Dr. Joyce Brothers
Fort Lee, New Jersey

Perhaps the most pernicious Expectation we drag into
marriage is the one holding "that a good marriage is one
that is smooth-running and best known for decorum, diplo-
macy, and dulcet tones." Now, fellow traveler, *where does
this belief stem from?*

Once again, we get an Expectation from the people who
gave you all the other Expectations: those friendly creators
of our myth-ridden society. This society maintains that life
is primarily a page out of a Loretta Young Charm School

rochure. Day-to-day marriage must be lived this way. The modus vivendi is "don't make waves," or "when entering the room, please walk on eggs."

But, as we all know, people cannot always be polite to each other, especially in day-in-and-day-out marriage. They have mood swings, bad backs, bad days (if not bad years) at the office.

What this Expectation obscures is that the smooth-as-silk, "yes, dear" relationship usually features one partner who goes underground, who swallows his anger daily and is quiet about it. Like some surly relative in a Dickens' novel, the underground partner is content to just sit there and collect grievances. When this kind of person is in a marriage that ultimately goes *phffttt!* the grievance collector invariably gets his courage back during the divorce proceedings and then displays total recall (sandbagging, as some of our experts call it.)

Now, our next question is: What happens if the marriage does not undergo any drastic changes? What if one grievance collector (but usually two) just sits there and keeps on collecting?

In many marriages, this cutoff and distanced style of relating to one another becomes a way of life. The couple made some deal between them never to rock the matrimonial boat, never to confront what is bothering them . . . not ever! They have only "Monday Night Football" on TV or their children's marriages to look forward to in their life together.

Let us now peruse the flip side. We are all familiar with the Virginia Woolf type of marriage—the Bickerson couple—those marrieds who use anger as a way of life. According to our above description, they should be our heroes. They are the ones who should be having the best kind of marriage. But, of course, they don't.

If the Bickersons of the world would admit some of their vulnerabilities and need for each other—if they could see that their fighting is a cover-up for their individual feelings of worthlessness or inadequacy—if they could realize that they could each be people in their own right *without* knocking someone else over the head to maintain this right—they might have a vital relationship.

They could give each other the attention they need by *caring*—not clobbering each other. Their anger does not belong with their partners. Experts tell us that this fury is usually over what they never got out of life—long before they ever knew the partner existed.

We have given examples of couples who do not bring their anger into the open, and those who leave it there all the time, living with it night and day. Is there a happy medium?

First, we must discuss a new kind of American marriage that, in the last few years, has become more and more popular. This kind is based toward keeping *absolutely nothing hidden*. It features such quaint imperatives as "self-expression," "letting it all hang out," and other modes of nonstop sonic boom too numerous to mention. This is hardly what anyone would call a "happy medium."

Although the open anger and confrontation might work in encounter and assertion groups, it doesn't quite succeed back at the old homestead. One partner always hears a 10,000-decibel request as an open attack and mentally starts running for the nearest soundproofed bunker. The victim becomes a helpless kid all over again, this anger reminding him all too well of the time he got bawled out by a parent.

The experts tell us that the nonstop sonic boom type of marriage works better than our charm school variety. They don't *recommend* it, mind you . . . but, nonetheless, it's better.

There is a terrible Catch 22 here. You are damned if you do express your anger and damned if you don't.

And now, in conclusion, some tips on "fair fighting." We'll take a typical argument and give it to you as an example. Let's take a couple who is angry over one or the other's behavior at parties—a common American bone of contention. Suppose *you* are talking. "I get uptight every time we go to the Smiths because you always do something to offend someone" is an honest statement. It tells your spouse that you are annoyed with his behavior, that it is really bugging you, and gives your mate a chance to do something about it the next time you dine with the Smiths. Nobody is condemning anybody or consigning the other to a psychiatric ward.

On the other hand, the statement "You are a hostile, narcissistic, insecure person who gets even with his rejecting mother by humiliating me in public" may be a profound example of psychological truth (let alone insight), but so what? This type of encountering makes your partner cringe and/or attack you with the weapons *he* has at hand or, even worse, *not* fight back but bury his rage somewhere in a sea of resentment. This kind of truthtelling is hardly getting you what you want.

You should take care of yourself first by practicing assertive but nonfighting sentences when you are having *any* kind of hassle. For example: "I'm going to visit my Aunt Tillie today and you're welcome to come along if you want to," or "We've discussed this thing about two thousand times before and I don't want to get stuck in it again." This way, your mate doesn't have to defend himself first by attacking you or drawing away from you in return. Using assertive methods, you're helping yourself as well as your mate. Nobody is hurt and both of you win.

We know all of this makes sense, but it isn't all that easy. It takes a long time to perfect the techniques of fair fighting.

But let's backtrack for a bit. How does one begin to express anger when one's mate doesn't know about "fair fighting"? Your voice is loud and your mate is cringing because, in his head, he thinks his parents are bawling him out once again. Our simple lesson? Take the bull by the horns and recognize that the bull is really a frightened calf.

Before airing the gripe, simply make a disclaimer. Start by saying something like, "I know my loud voice reminds you of your parents, but this is *me,* not a taped recording of them!" In this way, your partner will realize that you recognize him as a member of the human race and understand his problems.

When you try this disclaimer method a few times and realize that it generally does *get you heard,* your nonstop sonic booms will soon go beneath the 10,000-decibel range. Your wall groupings will stop jiggling and your neighbors upstairs can get back to their own quiet lives.

Does the Couple That Rarely Fights Have a Boring Marriage?

No, I don't think so. I think we have overused the idea of the importance of fighting in marriage. Now we have rules, we have referees and what happens when you do a great deal of fighting is that the fighting escalates. Even with rules, it doesn't seem to make a very satisfying marriage so that many people have worked out many ways of dealing with their quarrels or their adjustments.

I know one couple who saves everything for a whole week. They either write down or keep in their minds all of their arguments and they go out to dinner once a week and go over all their irritations and angers that have been built up for the whole week. Being out in public keeps them from beating up on each other. The restaurant itself, I imagine, has to be very fancy so that you can't shout too much.

And then they bring out all their grievances but, by the end of the week, they have discovered that the things that really mattered on Monday do not really seem all that important by Saturday and so that's their adjustment.

Another couple has a piece of paper and they put a line down the center and then they have two columns: HE SAYS and SHE SAYS. He makes his point and then she makes her interpretation of what he said, and vice versa. They find very often that what they are really talking about or arguing about is semantics. Many times they really mean the same thing. It's just there is a male kind of talk and a female kind of talk, and it's difficult to understand one another because they have been brought up in different ways.

Dr. Joyce Brothers
Fort Lee, New Jersey

I don't think it has anything to do with the marriage being boring. What matters most is the unconscious expectation about fighting, which is that this is a relationship and you have a commitment to one another. This means that all the troublesome issues are going to be discussed and that we are going to maintain our calm. We are going to reach a reasonable solution.

What actually happens, first of all, is that troublesome issues are not automatically brought up for the simple reason that, if you let sleeping dogs lie, perhaps you can get through without ever having them come up to the surface at all. This means that by the time they do get discussed, not only are they in a more aggravated state but now you have a whole lot of smaller sleeping dogs to rouse as well.

Another problem is that people don't always fight rationally. In fact, they *usually* don't fight rationally—that's the whole purpose of fighting.

It's also very rare that both partners will be on the same level of aggression or have the same tolerance level, so that what usually happens is that one partner (and it could be the man or the woman—often it is the man who has less tolerance) will withdraw. He simply stops fighting, he starts ignoring issues, he says, "I don't want to hear it." Sometimes women find that very threatening and feel that "he doesn't even care!" "He doesn't even want to discuss it!"

It may have nothing to do with his feelings about her; it's just the general way that he handles this sort of thing and, of course, the ultimate idea is that we are going to reach some solution—that there is an answer.

There is never a real answer. One of Tolstoy's

characters says, "One of you wants to go east and one of you wants to go west, so you wind up going north, which neither of you wanted at all." Sometimes that's the best type of solution. I think people have unrealistic expectations about fighting. Still, I think fighting can be a constructive thing. It's better to get things gently out in the open, even if it does involve a lot of heat.

Dr. William Appleton and
Jane Appleton
Cambridge, Massachusetts

Not necessarily. The question is where the state of not fighting much or not fighting at all comes from. My concern is what the underlying pattern is all about, what the psychodynamic is all about. It is interesting that we have to define *not* fighting as a state that is only relatively admirable. That should tell you something about the culture that we live in.

Fighting really stems from the fact that two people really have a good communication and what I call a "co-operative" relationship in which there is a good deal of mutual acceptance. That's certainly not boring.

Dr. Theodore Isaac Rubin
New York, New York

It's likely to be boring because they are keeping a lot of important things under wraps, and boredom is very often a cover for feelings that are not being expressed—often angry feelings, anxiety, are covered up with boredom. It's important to be able to have open and honest confrontations.

Bernard Berkowitz
New York, New York

No. I know couples who rarely fight and have very unboring marriages. Do you know something? There are as many ways, in my opinion, of being sexual as there are people in the world. And as there are days in the lives of each individual. Everything is different, every day.

Dr. Mary Calderone
Old Brookville, New York

No, not at all. Usually, passionate people do, among other things, once in a while passionately fight. Some interesting people do interesting things, including having a lot of interesting fights.

Dr. Albert Ellis
New York, New York

I would find it hard to believe that a couple didn't have disagreements, because if two people are unique, their differences have to show up somewhere. So I would start out with the business of differences, my discovery of difference in my mate, and his discovery of me. Now, depending on how we see that or hear that or use that, whether that will be something that we will be able to give and take with each other, whether we will have to try to put it away, deny it or get rid of it, we're going to have a dirty fight on our hands, and oftentimes that leads to bloodshed. We may have a lot of arguments, and we may have to do a lot of sharing and a lot of confronting so we can go somewhere with it. I have a hunch that unless there are some struggles, then there probably isn't that much uniqueness showing. You know, a lot of people have forgotten that the ability in a person to fight for himself or herself can relieve the other people from having to take care of them. And there are a lot of choices when it comes to fighting. You can sit there and baby yourself, and say how horrible it is. You can say what you feel, as many people don't. You can blame the other person. You can go and get yourself a nice fight going. Most of the time, people can go from one place to another when they feel they've got choices.

Dr. Virginia Satir
San Francisco, California

PART 2 OF THE TEST:
"FIGHTING"

Because many intimate relationships are based on the concept of "romantic" love, people feel that anger and arguments have no place in them. If an argument occurs or even if a partner feels an angry thought, some people feel this is a sign there is something basically wrong in their relationship.

However, when two people spend a lot of time together and have a great deal of emotional investment in each other, it is only natural that disagreements will occur from time to time.

If there is a basic confidence in the commitment of both partners to the relationship, the disagreements and anger are more easily dealt with and resolved.

This section of the test deals with how well you know how to handle your anger and whether you know how to *FIGHT* fairly.

Questions on "Fighting"

QUESTIONS:

Please circle T for those statements you think are true and F for those you think are false.

1. People usually argue about what really bothers them. T (F)

2. The longer you fight, the more likely you are to reach a permanent solution. T (F)

3. It's possible to have two winners in an argument. (T) F

4. It's best just to argue about one problem at a time and not bring up the past. (T) F

5. Fighting can actually lead to a better relationship. (T) F

SCORING:

For each correct answer, give yourself *10 points*.

MY SCORE FOR "FIGHTING" _____

Please turn the page for the correct answers.

Answers for
Part 2 of the Test: "Fighting"

---

1. *"People usually argue about what really bothers them."*

   FALSE

   Many times the real issue which is bothering a partner is avoided. A husband, after having a bad day at the office, may come home and begin to criticize the supper his wife has prepared. "Why don't you pay attention to what you're cooking—I get tired of burned pot roast!" he yells. They're off to a vehement argument on the wife's cooking skills when actually the husband is upset by the treatment he received from his boss that day. The put-down he got at work, he passes on at home.

2. *"The longer you fight, the more likely you are to reach a permanent solution."*

   FALSE

   Some couples fight for years over the same issues— money, smoking, in-laws, church attendance, swearing, sloppy housekeeping, interest in sports, etc.—and never resolve anything. Anger specialists call this kind of fighting a Round Robin Ritual. When a couple sees the destructiveness of this behavior to their relationship but can't seem to stop it themselves, they are prime candidates for counseling.

3. *"It's possible to have two winners in an argument."*

   TRUE

   Too often we approach arguing with a game mentality —someone has to win and someone has to lose. The effective way is to have no winner at all. When a couple realizes that the goal of a fight is to find a viable solution to a problem rather than to settle which person is right or wrong, arguments can be viewed in a new light. When the problem is solved or they have found a way to cope with the annoyance, they have both won.

4. *"It's best just to argue about one problem at a time and not bring up the past."*

   TRUE

   Specific grievances are more easily dealt with and more readily resolved than trying to deal with a multitude of issues at one time. All too often in an argument, a complaint by one partner triggers a countercriticism by the other. Soon, the main grievance is lost in a muddle of competing complaints. Bringing up past hurts means that they haven't been successfully resolved and will only cloud the issue at hand. Deal with the here and now, since the facts of the past cannot be changed. Attitudes toward them and memories of them, fortunately, can.

5. *"Fighting can actually lead to a better relationship."*

   TRUE

   Absence of disagreement doesn't necessarily mean a relationship is a strong one. People who are insecure about their standing with their partners or who have little investment in the relationship may seek to avoid arguments or disputes. What really matters is *how* the partners disagree. When difficulties are truly resolved to the satisfaction of both partners, when the decision has not been made unilaterally or forced upon one of the mates, the overcoming of such difficulties can strengthen and improve a relationship.

SCORING:

   Give yourself 10 points for each "False" response to questions 1 and 2. Give yourself 10 points for each "True" response to questions 3, 4, and 5.

EVALUATION:

The higher your score, the more fairly you fight and the more likely you are to be able to solve difficulties in your relationship.

4

EXPECTATION ⌗3:

that sex will be limitless in an ongoing relationship

What my dream would be for the people of this country, the United States, is that they would become the same type of people that Margaret Mead wrote of so early in our youth in the lovely dream world of Samoa—gentle, warm, straight and honest, intelligent, nonexploitative in all of their dealings. Then you would not have to worry about sex.

Dr. Mary Calderone
Old Brookville, New York

We all know that we are in the middle of a sexual revolution and that there is more sexual knowledge around than ever before. The only thing that really hasn't changed all that much is the secret, unconscious male Expectations of sex.

Friend Male still enters marriage, takes these secret Expectations, and puts them in the form of a *contract*.

HIS CONTRACT:

I, John Doe, being of sound body and mind, have contracted for an unlimited supply of sex, of the variety and amount that I choose. You, of course, will be pleased to supply it. Signed, sealed, and to be delivered by United Parcel.

We of THE NATIONAL LOVE, SEX & MARRIAGE TEST will now investigate how he got that way. We of THE NATIONAL LOVE, SEX & MARRIAGE TEST, although not wishing to blame anyone, feel that the males' cultural conditioning is the problem. Although things are changing now, how males were raised and how they view sex is where 50 per cent of the trouble lies. We will call this 50 per cent "male nonsexual motivations for sex."

The experts tell us that a man's sexual needs are not always really *sexual* needs. They might be problems which haven't yet surfaced so they could be identified and recognized. Yet many experts tell us that underlying our high divorce rate are these male expectations that are placed in the form of a secret contract. The husband, in the grand old American tradition, married someone to give him limitless sex and it simply doesn't work out. Women are becoming in tune with their own needs; they are no longer happy to be the sexual "pleasers."

Now to the issue! As we said, the problem with a marriage based primarily on a man's sexual needs is that at least 50 per cent of the people involved in it don't really know that they have signed a contract to please the other. Deep down, on some very subconscious level, the man knows it, but he would never muster the guts to come right out and say that to his beloved. No man on this planet could be honest on that point. It is only after the woman starts withdrawing her availability (first sexual, then emotional) that the problem surfaces in living color.

She wants to please—her mother told her she should—but after a while (usually the first year of marriage), she can't stand the strain and begins to wonder why she "should" in the first place.

It is at this point when the woman changes ever so slightly that your male Expectation Buff begins to feel neglected—he is not getting what he hoped for in the relationship. Then we're off to the races! The recriminations start snowballing and both people eventually wind up feeling shortchanged.

In short, we are going to help the male face a very central issue in his life: *His sexual problems are not sex.* Most of a man's primary sexual motivations have absolutely nothing to do with the purely sensual pleasures of the flesh. So, as a special service (to men and women), we will unmask some of the main masquerades, and be done with it once and for all.

THE VALIDATED PARKING MOTIVATION

Our first nonsexual motivation for sex in males we call the Validated Parking Check Feeling. Purely and simply, men use sex to feel that they belong—to be a member of the club, to be accepted.

They feel that if the woman will accommodate their sexual desires at all times (regardless of whether or not the latter is desirous of sex), it is proof-positive that they are worthy of being loved.

For a man, there is nothing quite like the warm feelings stemming from a loving sexual experience to make him feel that God's in his heaven, all's right with the world. It can be compared to the feeling one gets when receiving validation for a parking check, even though an actual purchase has not been made. The man feels valuable and wanted—*just* for *being*.

Note: This undoubtedly explains why there are more successful parking lots than sexually compatible marriages.

THE GARY COOPER (OR
CLINT EASTWOOD) SYNDROME

Then there's the Gary Cooper Syndrome. We're sure most of the readers are old enough to remember the kind of folk hero the late Gary Cooper (and now Clint Eastwood) played in all those Western movies. He was the strong, silent, withdrawn type, who said "Yup" a lot and, in some rare situations, "Huh?"

In any event, this tuned-out macho type represented some kind of American Masculine Ideal—the kind of mysterious, nonverbal Prince Charming who shoots first and then is too shy to ask questions later.

For a man who has difficulty relating to a woman verbally or emotionally, his sex organ becomes an instrument of communication. It acts as a sort of conversational icebreaker and becomes the only means he has of achieving any kind of closeness with a woman.

THE DON JUAN COMPLEX

Now let's discuss the best-known nonsexual motivation for sex. Renowned in opera, celebrated in literature, replayed in movies too numerous to mention—Don Juanism. We are sure the reader is familiar with it: the need to see how many different women a man can capture in a given tax quarter.

Experts we've talked to hold that this particular instability or compulsion stems from the weird drive some men have to *conquer* women rather than to achieve genuine relationships with them. Or, to borrow from our own nonscientific terminology, that they need excessive Parking Check Validations because they have been voided inside.

We've heard one explanation for this, from an analyst in

Beverly Hills, which we considered highly original and intriguing. According to him, the typical Don Juan is motivated by a secret fantasy many men have—that he's going to see something different each time a different woman undresses before him.

There is one issue, however, that all the experts seem to be in complete agreement on. Men afflicted with this problem may be very celebrated in literature and film but, in reality, they present a very pathetic picture.

Their world is a kind of free-floating hell in which nothing is ever enough and where nothing truly satisfies them. Whatever it is that they have now, it is never as good as what they are going to have.

THE ORGASM COLLECTOR

Another type, closely associated with "Don Juan," is the Orgasm Collector. Men addicted to winning prizes in sales contests or to making *Law Review* in college are concerned with only one thing when it comes to sex: to prove *their own adequacy* by seeing how many orgasms they can "elicit" from their partners. The primary concern is not in getting (much less in giving) pleasure, but in "scoring" brownie points for their psyche.

Sex is always an "on-stage," "do-or-die" performance for them. However, in order to perform, they have a whole collection of performance-prolonging mental games which they play (with themselves) during the sex act—things like: (a) the win/loss record of the Minnesota Vikings during the 1959 season; (b) capital gains schedules for their stock purchases over the last ten years; or (c) what the status was of their oil filter during the last 5,000-mile check-up.

The problem for the Orgasm Collector's partner, of course, is obvious. She feels more like a spectator than a participant—a scoreboard for his psyche rather than a loving sex partner.

THE MADONNA COMPLEX

The Madonna Complex transpires when men find sex difficult with their wives because, after marriage, their wives become less available to them. For one reason or another, children's routines, dinners, sexual tune-outs, and back-to-back nocturnal headaches make sex seem forbidden.

Ergo, men trying to deal with their disappointment often find that they can perform with other women who do not cull up this "Mother," "White Maiden," "Madonna-like" image. These women often include anonymous types like prostitutes, bar pick-ups, etc., and other varieties who do not scream for a police rescue squad the second they feel they are being sexually "used."

The treatment for the male afflicted with this malady? Unfortunately, the sufferer does not know that if he recycled and reprogrammed that mother figure in his head, he would find that sex can be just as exciting at home as it can be in any other location. By changing some of his notions and fantasies, he could turn his own wife into a highly satisfactory sex partner. Naturally, it takes a little co-operation from the Madonna figure herself. She has to stop behaving like a Madonna and explore some of her own sexual needs, and take some responsibility for the sexual relationship.

SATURDAY NIGHT SEX

According to experts, our final example is representative of a large part of the American population: couples who practice Ritualized Sex.

The husband will, without any carnal craving whatsoever, experience a light bulb going off in his brain telling him that six days have elapsed and the time has finally rolled around again for Sexual Intercourse. By now, you

can surely recognize this motivation as yet another variation of the Ovaltine Syndrome, in that the husband has little or no involvement emotionally, per se. He only knows
that, sex-wise, it will be "good for him."

Most problems arise, however, when the man feels that
relating sexually to his mate in this way is his right. His
gilt-edged expectation, her duty-bound obligation. Then
the woman feels like a sexual slave and starts retaliating in
all sorts of covert, passive-aggressive ways.

Our most important point: *This ritualized use of sex is
just as much the woman's responsibility as her mate's.* In
other words, it takes the co-operation of two people to
allow meaningless sex to continue *pro forma.*

So much for the problem.

What do the experts advise for people who want to turn
this condition around? What should couples do in order to
have their real sexual needs recognized instead of living
out the syndromes that we've just discussed?

What Is the Most Dangerous and False Expectation About Sex in Marriage?

I think the most false expectation people can have regarding sex is to expect any kind of specific performance. That's what I think is the most false thing. Many people don't realize that sex is like talk, like conversation, that you do a step at a time, and there are always two people involved and then there is the action that's going on between them and that this differs in every situation. It differs with where each person is and it is a growing kind of thing that differs situation by situation, and there are no demands around it. It's like a treasure that you evolve. As you can imagine, in over forty years, I've had plenty of men talk to me about their sex lives, and one of the things that men tell me, too, is, "I can't live up to the feeling that I must always perform. I feel there is no rational reason why I should, and many times, I don't want to. And it doesn't have anything to do with loving. My energy may not be with my sexual self at this point." And then, there is another part to it, and that has to do with what many men have said to me: "Why can't women have more fun? Why can't this be more fun for me?" You know, many people feel that sex is either an unnecessary thing, or that it is something that one pays to want or that one gets as a reward. And when you're using it at the bargaining table like that, or when you're using it to define who two people are in a relationship, you can't have fun with it. It gets too heavy into the survival thing to be fun.

Dr. Virginia Satir
San Francisco, California

If I had to center on one thing, I would say it's unrealistic to expect the other person's sex expectation to be the same as yours. You're going to have to negotiate good sex. You can't assume that good sex for you would be good sex for them. It has to be negotiated.

Carlfred B. Broderick, Ph.D.
Los Angeles, California

I think the *stated* provision, going in, is that you will give me sex whenever I want it—from the male point and I think from the female point, too. However, in the past, women were not usually the aggressors. They did not say, "I would like sex tonight," or send out any kind of signals. And what often happens in a relationship is that, really, people don't get sex every time they want it. They start giving out little signals, "I'm not in the mood tonight," "I'm not receptive." People don't like direct advances in a marriage or a living-together relationship. You have your own little set of signals and you begin to communicate this: "Leave me alone tonight," "Well, maybe you could persuade me, although I would really rather not," "Try me in a couple of hours." The initial expectation is that "we will never deny each other sex," but it actually works out a little differently, because what you are finding out is that you have all sorts of little signals. The other thing is that men today are much more concerned about pleasing their partners. A man can't go in there and say, "Well, I enjoyed myself." So much of his own feelings about himself depend on,

"Can I satisfy my woman?" "Is she happy, too?" And it can totally ruin the whole experience for him if he feels that she's cold, that she's disinterested."

Anthony Pietropinto, M.D.
New York, New York

Well, the most dangerous of expectations, and certainly the most destructive, is that each person ought to *know* what the other person wants without any kind of verbal communication. Many people engage in a "conspiracy with silence," and I might say a silent conspiracy with silence, because they don't even talk about it with each other, very often for forty, fifty years of marriage, a lifetime—never telling each other just what it is they like, don't like, or what ought to be done. And this is on the claim, "If you love me, you ought to know," and "I ought not to have to tell you," and "If I have to tell you, then the whole thing is not adequate, it destroys the entrancing romance," and so forth. Of course, people do talk about sex, especially in sustained relationships like marriage, more than they ever did. But I still see any number of people who do not talk about their life's wants, needs, and so forth.

Dr. Theodore Isaac Rubin
New York, New York

I think the most dangerous idea is to feel that sex can express all of your needs and wants and desires. Sex is really a bridge. If you care for the person, it expresses this feeling of concern to go over that bridge. If you feel hostile toward the other person, the sex will be aggressive and mean and hostile. So in our society, we feel that we are *owed* sexual gratification, much like the commercial where a man puts some stuff on his hair and women come out of the wood-work and attack him. Well, people feel that if they groom themselves and put on the right deodorant, per-fume, and so on, the opposite sex will attack them. Well, it isn't so. We only get out of sex what we put into it. But it does come back gift-wrapped.

Dr. Joyce Brothers
Fort Lee, New Jersey

If their expectations of sex include expecting that it will solve all of their interpersonal problems, they had better forget that. It's a crime to load on this one sim-ple, beautiful relationship between two people all of the problems of a marriage and, if there is one thing I would say, it is, "Don't do that." Don't load onto sex your expectations that it will solve your interpersonal problems of living with another person.

Dr. Mary Calderone
Old Brookville, New York

Lying—seducing the person that you're with by not telling him that you have needs. I have seen women, as well as men, in my practice who really get into trouble because they tell their partner they don't need anything; they have led them to believe they were going to give them everything, they were going to feed them totally, and that they did not need to be fed. Each of us needs. And each of us wants. And you have to be able to admit that you want, that you need, that you care, that you have to have things, and that you want to get them. You have to take chances. We come back to courage. You have to have the convic-tion of what you believe in. You have to know that you are human and that you need things. No matter how big and strong you are, you need things—you need someone to love and someone to love you, to baby you sometimes, and to give you all kinds of things.

Mildred Newman
New York, New York

Well, I think the biggest booby trap is taking the other person, the situation, and love for granted. Whether you are talking about sex or life in general, this is true. It's a little bit like living on an incline plane—you can't stand still, because you will slide down; things that stand still stagnate, they deteriorate; love is an act; love is not passive. If you take it for granted and just assume that the other person is going to be there somehow or another, then things are likely to stagnate and deteriorate. But if you bring to it a certain degree of creativity, love or marriage or life can be almost anything you want to make of it.

The creative part comes in not only expressing your own needs—being honest enough to be vulnerable and open and say, "This is what I need"—but also to listen attentively to what your partner is saying so that you tune in on those needs of your partner that are not easily and readily expressed. And to think of the creative ways of satisfying and gratifying those needs. Well, if they cannot be asked, and if you can fathom them anyhow, then you are all right.

Bernard Berkowitz
New York, New York

Do Women Have an Easier Time Satisfying Their Sexual Needs Than Men Do?

I think neither. Women, I have found, even very sexually active women, will often go through their nunnery periods; they will often go three, four months without a man and say, "I never really missed it," and then all of a sudden they are back out on the circuit. And I think that, on the other hand, a man has to sort of pull his head together with his genital drive, and he may feel, "Well, I have a physical need for sex, but I haven't really got a partner that I can get my head to jive with." And, in that sense, a man forgoes sex because he doesn't want to go with a woman just for the sake of having sex, because he just didn't have it all together.

Anthony Pietropinto, M.D.
New York, New York

Not necessarily, because women don't allow themselves to and some of them, more than men, have a hard time thinking their way and acting their way into heights of orgasm. So they often have to work harder and just refuse to work at it.

Dr. Albert Ellis
New York, New York

I suspect, despite all that men say or women think they say or hear them say, that men are so active in being able to get their sexual needs met, that a lot of this is untrue. I know there is a lot of sexual acting out, because men are basically very often shy and fear being rejected. But I don't think they get as much as people think they do. I think that men may have had more—maybe it is a permission sort of thing—permission to masturbate and get things out of pornography and things like that. I'm going on my clinical hunches here, as I haven't done any research on this. But I think more or less that many women have probably had an easier time. I think the woman is likely to be a little more covert. But there are many difficulties for men and women. What's interesting, however, is that ever since the Kinsey report—which opened up lots more opportunity to learn about things, though I don't know that it freed many people *inside*—I think both men and women took different kinds of action. We learned more about the dissatisfactions that were going on, for *both* sexes.

Dr. Virginia Satir
San Francisco, California

From the very beginning, males are penis-oriented. That's where it is. That is part of the relatively simple sexual mechanism of the male who is built to respond instantly. And, in contrast, females—not just human females but also females of the lower animals—have to go through a period of courtship, in which there is a readiness engaged in and prepared for. That's one of the differences. And I think many women do feel that way. I don't think either men or women have an easy time about sex, these days. They still don't know how to communicate about it.

Dr. Mary Calderone
Old Brookville, New York

In our culture, we know women have a harder time. Many more women, whether you take their self-report of satisfaction or you take orgasm as a criterion, have a harder time achieving satisfaction than men do. Kinsey, I think, misconcluded that the reason was biological. He made statements which I think are totally wrong, such as, "Women mature more slowly than men," "They're into their forties before they reach their sexual maturity," and so on—I think this is nonsense. I think we teach women—or have, until this generation, taught women—*not* to be in touch with their own sexuality and not even to recognize it. Women, for example, who masturbate and do not know it or call it by that name with any sexual connotation, don't have any sexual fantasies associated with it. They don't connect it with romance or with men. It's just sort of an absent-minded fingering of the genitals that is much closer to something like biting your fingernails. Males are not permitted that. The sexual implications of an erection, for example, are immediately pointed out to a male. He's not permitted to have a nonsexual erection, although an erection is just a physiological experience. It is defined. What we could call "sexual scripts" are imposed upon the male much more enthusiastically and comprehensively than they are on the female. So, for that reason, I think that very few males are out of touch with their sexuality and, perhaps today in decreasing numbers, women. But there's still no question that the advantage is with the males in terms, simply, of their accepting and being familiar with their bodies, the fact that they are sexual creatures, and what it takes to stimulate them sexually.

Carlfred B. Broderick, Ph.D.
Los Angeles, California

What Is Your Definition of "Promiscuous" Sex?

I don't use the word "promiscuous" myself, because first of all I think it's a sexist kind of a term. It's the kind of a term that traditionally has been applied to women who have had random sexual contacts, where we call men who have had the same number and kind of contacts "studs" or "experienced" or "bon vivants," or something like that. I try to avoid the use of that. I think what is important to me in a relationship, of a narrow, sexual kind, is who the people are, how they feel, being in the experience, the motives that bring them there, what they derive from the experience. I try to make my judgments, if I'm in that position, about the relationship based on those kinds of things, rather than arbitrary standards which have been set up by other people. There are some people who can become involved genitally with other people in a very candid and honest way which is not exploitive and not self-destructive, but it's not going to lead to some long-term relationship. And there are many other people who really have to have a kind of emotional involvement and a committed relationship before intercourse or genital sex has any meaning or fits within that relationship. But, regardless of the circumstances, I very rarely, if ever, will use the term "promiscuous."

Dr. Michael Carrera
New York, New York

I suppose it might be valuable to make a distinction between frequent sex with many partners on the one hand and sex which, however thoughtfully it is engaged in, is also called "promiscuous" sex. This second type I am more concerned about as a therapist— where a person through sexual behavior shows very little respect for themselves. For example, even though they didn't like someone, didn't want to be with them, didn't want to have sex with them, they would feel obligated to do so because of the situation or because of the importunity of the other person or whatever. I would call sex promiscuous where there is no judgment involved, no self-regard, no self-protection.

Carlfred B. Broderick, Ph.D.
Los Angeles, California

I think anybody who does the sexual act for reasons other than wanting to share intimacy and caring about someone is promiscuous. I know people who, for them, it's the same as driving up to an ice-cream stand and ordering ice cream. They go out and have sex.

Jane Appleton
Cambridge, Massachusetts

To me, it's a sexual relationship that does not include love. The moment a person feels love for someone or feels loved by someone, it takes on the coloration of the family—it takes on the feeling about the mother and/or the father. And it's too much to bear. So you have to work it out (and it doesn't have to be in analysis of any kind—you can do that for yourself), you have to know that you feel that way, and work through those feelings. It doesn't have to go on and on.

Mildred Newman
New York, New York

The promiscuous person is the person who has had sex with one more person than you have. And I don't use the term "promiscuous." I recognize as a physician that there is such a thing as compulsive promiscuity and that there are roots for compulsive promiscuity, which are deprivation of affection in early years—and I know a number of young people who are promiscuous who had this kind of deprivation in their youngest childhood years and are acting this out now, later—so I would hesitate ever to apply the term. It's a condition—like alcoholism—which must be treated.

Dr. Mary Calderone
Old Brookville, New York

I'll tell you what the word means to me. It's people who have a sexual contact without relevance to whether or not they have a relationship with the person or are interested in that person. It's like a mechanical kind of business. That would be my definition.

Dr. Virginia Satir
San Francisco, California

What Do You Think of
a Sexless Marriage?

I don't condemn it, but the question comes down to a definition of a marriage and of a relationship. And it's possible to have a very fruitful and sustained relationship without sex, but it certainly does not define our concept of what a marriage is about. Can it work on some kind of fruitful level? I think it depends upon the kind of people involved. On what their expectations are, what their value systems are. If you have two relatively asexual people, it's possible; if you have an individual who is not asexual and another person who is . . . well, there has got to be trouble there.

Dr. Theodore Isaac Rubin
New York, New York

I once wrote a paper on marriage without sex, and I showed that many marriages, after a while, have very little or no sex and can still be good human relationships. Not preferably so, they also had the sex, but they don't need it in order to have a good marriage.

Dr. Albert Ellis
New York, New York

I think that there can be some very splendid sexless marriages, where two people have other kinds of needs that they fulfill in one another. We don't all have the same sex drive. There seems to be a primary difference, for example, where some people are born with a lower sex drive than others; you also have differences because of events that occur in our lifetime. Some people have been terrified of sex, or they have been brought up without any love and so they don't know how to give love, or they have been pressured into sex at too early an age so that they have not fused the feeling of love and sex into one person —they can have love with one person and sex with another. People can live a lifetime without sex. The body takes care of its own needs, in sexual dreams, for example. And there are husbands and wives who live like brothers and sisters, but they have many other interests in common so their marriage survives. I think the A-※1 best marriages are marriages which fuse love and sex, where the two people enjoy each other. They like each other as well as love each other and have a great sex life.

Dr. Joyce Brothers
Fort Lee, New Jersey

Well, it depends. Some marriages are sexless because people have never been able to consummate their marriage—for whatever reasons. I haven't seen any marriages like that which are very happy, and I would think that the sexual energy is very important for a relationship between two people. It would be kind of hard for me to see that there could be some completeness when a marriage is totally sexless—except maybe when people have become so evolved as people up into the higher consciousness. Perhaps then it would be a different thing. I feel puzzled about marriages like this. I wonder, what does the personality do to itself, and how does it work it out with itself so that it can have even a modicum of feeling whole?

Dr. Virginia Satir
San Francisco, California

With people who choose to have no intercourse, if it's something they feel comfortable with, something that they are honest about, and have communicated about, something they have decided, then I don't have any problem with it. If it really springs from within, either the way they relate or the lack of relating is comfortable for both of them, then I would not consider that a pejorative thing in a relationship.

Dr. Michael Carrera
New York, New York

I don't know. I've never tried one. But if it's right for them, why not? I don't believe it's for me, but why not for them if they believe in it and it is right for them. It can happen.

Dr. Mary Calderone
Old Brookville, New York

I think something very important is left out. It makes me feel very sad to think of a sexless marriage. I think these people are inhibited and blocked from being with each other and loving each other as fully as possible. It may be a very satisfying relationship in other ways, but something important is missing.

Bernard Berkowitz
New York, New York

I know some happy sexless *people,* but I don't know any happy sexless marriages. I know people who only make it once a year . . . but they're not happy. Why would they come to me to tell me they're happy? However, in cases where it's not voluntary, but because of some biologically induced impotency on the part of the male, couples have resigned the sexual part of their marriage. Everything else was so good and, while they don't rejoice that they're not having sex, they don't let it mar the rest of a good relationship. I don't know anyone with a happy marriage where one partner unilaterally withholds sex that they would be capable of giving, if they would.

Carlfred B. Broderick, Ph.D.
Los Angeles, California

*What Have You Found
to Be the Greatest Source of Problems
in Sexual Relationships?*

The greatest source of sexual problems, I think, is mismatched scripts—where people don't have the same scripts and don't *know,* don't recognize the problem as being a problem. They're doing all the things they know how to do and their mate is not responding and it never *occurs* to them that there's any other script than the one in their heads. It may sound foolish, but they've read it in a book or heard it from a good authority, or their first wife loved it or their first husband was turned on by it, and it literally does not occur to them that there is another, different script. That, by itself, would be negotiable, if they recognized that that's what they were doing. But it's the blindness to that fact—it's the puzzlement and the hurt when they find that the things that they do that are *supposed* to be guaranteed to turn on a spouse (or that it surely would if they loved them or cared about them) are not working. Sometimes it's not even that they assume the other person should enjoy what they give; it's that they're waiting for a cue for their entry, and they don't get the cue. They're waiting for the touch, the look, the invitation, the whatever, that triggers responses in them and their spouse doesn't do that thing, whatever it is, or say those words.

They choose to ignore each other's script out of a power struggle because, although they often know what the partner means, it does not satisfy their *own* script. It's not *the* cue that they choose to respond to. They reject a cue which was perfectly clear in its intent because it was not a cue in their own script. Fortunately, a minority of couples are this badly mis-scripted and so without resources in finding joint scripts that they just can't get it together—what we label "dysfunctional."

Carlfred B. Broderick, Ph.D.
Los Angeles, California

I would say competitiveness is the greatest source of problems in sexual relationships.

Ann Landers
Chicago, Illinois

I would say that control is one of the prime sources of sexual problems. For example, any situation where sex is used as a control or where other issues in the relationship are under a type of control which makes for little opportunity, really, to come together in a joyful situation. "I'm married to you, therefore . . . ," or, "You're my wife, therefore you have to . . . ," or, "This is my duty, and I have to . . . ," are examples of controls in a relationship. The problems I find are usually in the area of communication. As a matter of fact, I can hear people communicate with one another and pretty much tell what they do in bed.

Dr. Virginia Satir
San Francisco, California

PART 3 OF THE TEST:
"SEX"

The degree to which sexuality was a taboo subject is illustrated by the fact that, even as late as 1940, the New York *Times* declined an ad for Kinsey's *Sexual Behavior of the Human Male*.

With the development of reliable contraception, changing definitions of male and female roles, and increasing interest in personal development and self-fulfillment, we have seen a greater acceptance of sexuality in general and women's sexuality in particular.

However, many people still find it difficult to communicate openly with their partners their feelings about this area of human expression.

In this section of the test, the degree to which you are open about and how well you understand the role of *SEX* in a relationship will be measured.

Questions on "Sex"

QUESTIONS:

Please circle the letter which best describes your feelings about each of the following questions.

1. Hugging and cuddling are:
   A) not important if people really love each other.
   B) important and different from making love.
   C) only important before making love.

2. Sexual fantasies, or daydreams:
   A) make a love relationship more exciting.
   B) show there is something missing in your relationship.
   C) lead to sex crimes.

3. The main responsibility for birth control should be with:
   A) the woman.
   B) the man.
   C) both mates together.

4. When making love:
   A) people naturally know what to do.
   B) you have to tell your mate what is pleasing.

5. As the years pass, I expect that my love life with my partner will:
   A) fade away.
   B) become less satisfying.
   C) improve.

6. The most common difficulty in a loving relationship is:
   A) money problems.

   Ⓑ communication problems.
   C) physical incompatibility.

SCORING:

For each correct answer, give yourself *10 points*.

MY SCORE FOR "SEX"_____

Please turn the page for the correct answers.

Answers for
Part 3 of the Test: "Sex"

---

1. *"Hugging and cuddling are:*
   A) not important if people really love each other.
   B) important and different from making love.
   C) only important before making love."

   THE CORRECT ANSWER IS: (B)

   "Body language" expresses tenderness and affection in ways that words often cannot. Although some people are touchers and others are not, usually because of early family experiences, nearly all of us need the warmth of loving contact from infancy on. Intercourse alone may be insufficient to fill these contact needs.

2. *"Sexual fantasies, or daydreams:*
   A) make a love relationship more exciting.
   B) show there is something missing in your relationship.
   C) lead to sex crimes."

   THE CORRECT ANSWER IS: (A)

   It has been said that the largest sex organ in the body is the brain. Most (if not all) sexual behaviors are responses to what is going on in our heads. Both impotence and sexual adequacy are closely linked to the imagery in a person's mind. Fantasies don't mean that the fantasizer is rejecting a partner or that the behavior fantasized is actually intended to become action. Fantasies may indeed be a way to stimulate new and exciting thoughts and behaviors related to one's partner.

3. *"The main responsibility for birth control should be with:*

A) the woman.
B) the man.
C) both mates together."

THE CORRECT ANSWER IS: (C)

Mutual agreement on contraception is a way of showing a commitment to and a respect for one's partner. Certainly both partners should be concerned with their own and their mate's aesthetics, convenience, freedom from annoyance, and feelings of mutuality in this most intimate form of communication.

4. *"When making love:*
   A) people naturally know what to do.
   B) you have to tell your mate what is pleasing."

THE CORRECT ANSWER IS: (B)

There are identifiable stages in love-making from excitement and arousal through to "afterglow" and resolution that are made more or less satisfying by the kinds of stimulation that are taking place. If either partner doesn't find some way to guide the other, then their interaction has to be based on guesswork or "mind reading" about what stage the partner is in. No technique can be guaranteed to be effective all the time, but guesswork is almost never effective.

5. *"As the years pass, I expect that my love life with my partner will:*
   A) fade away.
   B) become less satisfying.
   C) improve."

THE CORRECT ANSWER IS: (C)

The common assumption that either aging or long continuation of a relationship causes a decline in libidinal drives or sexual satisfaction has been shown to be fallacious. Even though frequency of intercourse may decline with passing years, satisfaction may in fact improve, both as a result of learning better sexual techniques and as a result of fulfillment in the over-all relationship.

6. *"The most common difficulty in a loving relationship is:*
   A) money problems.
   B) communication problems.
   C) physical incompatibility."

THE CORRECT ANSWER IS: (B)

The Family Service Association of America found in a 1975 study that over 80 per cent of the persons coming for counseling reported that their chief problem was communication. Much lower percentages reported that they had money problems or sex problems.

SCORING:

Give yourself 10 points if you marked response "A" for question 2. Give yourself 10 points for each "B" response to questions 1, 4, and 6. Give yourself 10 points for each "C" response to questions 3 and 5.

EVALUATION:

The higher your score, the more open you are about your own sexuality and the more likely you are to have a satisfying sexual relationship.

5

EXPECTATION #4:

that instant communication comes with the territory

The most dangerous of expectations, and certainly the most destructive, is that each person ought to *know* what the other person wants without any kind of verbal communication. I think that people who engage in a "conspiracy with silence," and I might say a silent conspiracy with silence, because they don't even talk about it with each other, very often for forty, fifty years of marriage, a lifetime—never telling each other just what it is they like, don't like, or what ought to be done. And this is on the claim "If you love me, you ought to know," and "I ought not to have to tell you," and "If I have to tell you, then the whole thing is not adequate, it destroys the entrancing romance," and so forth.

Dr. Theodore Isaac Rubin
New York, New York

Now we are ready to talk about a very difficult subject—which, familiar as it is, we find the most difficult of all areas in our test to talk about: "Feelings" . . . but, more importantly, how to communicate them.

Let us turn now to the malaise that is supposed to occur when a relationship is bereft of feelings and open communication. As yet another invaluable service of THE NATIONAL LOVE, SEX & MARRIAGE TEST, herein follow some of the danger signals:

Symptom ⚹1:

Not enough personal conversation of the kind that leads to the Real Intimacy. Your talk—yours and your beloved's, that is—is surface and lifeless. Where you begin noticing that, although your mate is a regular bon vivant with everyone else, things certainly change when it comes to you. The two of you can be mumbling something to each other over breakfast, but the minute the phone rings and the other answers it, his voice becomes animated and alive. You, the victim, suddenly find yourself wishing you were the "other person" on the telephone.

Symptom ⚹2:

You feel moods of sadness and emptiness in the relationship that descend upon you from almost out of nowhere, especially when you are alone, and particularly on vacations. One day, you get tired of telling yourself that marriage is "just that way," and you know that something is missing. You feel cheated, and it is about something very specific. But what is it?

Symptom ⚹3:

You are indifferent to each other's problems and interests. When one of you tells the other about something *awful* that has happened on the outside, no one is there to provide a sympathetic ear. There is simply no comforting interest on anybody's part. In response to the other person's recounting of the "disaster," we, parties of the second part, can always be mature and reasonable. What the other person wants is blind, primitive loyalty, of the kind and class only the Mafia knows. But what actually happens is that we swathe our wounded partners with logic.

Symptom #4:

You feel disillusioned and bored with your relationship. You know the other's responses before there are any questions. Forgive us, gentle readers, for sounding cornball, but there is none of that old excitement about discovering each other and, after a certain point, nothing more is revealed about either one of you. When you talk about doing something for fun, it's always in terms of doing it with other couples. Let's face it, if we weren't married, we would be the last ones we would ever call up for lunch.

Symptom #5:

You don't fight fairly. Forget *fairly*. Most fights end with one person walking out of the room and, if no one happens to walk out of the room, one of you will superficially agree, and maybe say you're sorry, and then clam up behind some kind of phony shell—which is, as we all know, far worse than simply walking out of the room. Your hassles lead to other hassles, rather than to any real insights.

Symptom #6:

Both of you do such a good job of blame-laying and putting the other down—both in public and in private—that you reinforce the supremely bad images you have of yourselves—those awful parts of yourselves that were so endearing when you first met and are now being exposed blatantly to each other whenever a grand opportunity arises. No wonder both of you feel better *anywhere else* than you do at home.

Symptom #7:

There has been a famine of the signs of courtesy, gentleness, and caring. You have both lost the ability to idolize and be romantic about each other and to provide inspiration for each other's projects. You are too depleted most of the time to feel like giving. There are no more fun cards to give, goofy love tokens, or "just for nothing" presents to receive. In fact, even buying the ritual birthday and anniversary gifts has become just that—ritual.

Symptom #8:

Other people—friends, relatives, people you meet at bus stops—listen and understand you better than your mate. They know who you are, *really*. As a couple, however, there is always a kind of angry disappointment underneath everything you do. And sometimes the slightest little thing can turn into a huge argument—one that surprises you with its vehemence. To avoid these eruptions, you have to be phony and guarded a lot of the time, and you must keep mental lists of "forbidden topics" so you don't step on each other's toes. You know you have reached the bottom-line symptom of bad communication when you have the feeling you are walking on eggs all the time.

Symptom #9:

You feel in a rut. You spend a good portion of your time daydreaming about being in some other relationship. You keep fantasizing about having sex with other people. When you are not taking each other for granted, you have this clingy feeling of being extensions of each other—like "Frick and Frack." You are always at your best for other people and save the worst for when you come home. Your relationship is not a haven; it's a dumping ground.

What we are saying is that all of these symptoms spell one thing: *bad communication*. You no longer have that original empathy for one another; you have lost the ability to put yourselves in each other's skin. You can't reach out to the other.

We Americans really believe that a good marriage (one with clear communication) will cure loneliness. Isn't that really the heart of this whole communication obsession? Where did we get the idea that a good relationship will cure our individual loneliness? It comes with the territory!

What about marrying a person you have a lot in common with so you won't feel lonely? The kind of relationship based on similar life-styles, shared intellectual pursuits, and identical goals and values? It's our contention that it's no better cure for loneliness than most other kinds of marriages.

Why? Well, take somebody who is lonely but experiences boredom and restlessness. A woman might marry a man who will take her everywhere and keep her entertained most of the time. This works during courtship beautifully—as a kind of recreation—but, after a few years of marriage, the husband can't stand the pressure of pleasing her day after day, of entertaining her 100 per cent of the time. Although this might sound like a broken record, it bears repeating and repeating: *Expectations almost always do us in.* The person who thought his companion in marriage would help him to escape from loneliness feels terribly deprived when he's still lonely. The fantasy has been shattered. The mate, once again, has broken the provisions of a contract he didn't even know he'd signed.

Any marriage that doesn't take care of a strong need, especially one as pervasive as loneliness, won't work. The minute one partner decides not to satisfy the needs of the other, the relationship is in danger of going *poof!*

Everybody is afflicted with loneliness. What the lonely Expectation Buff must learn is how to hook up with *other* people who are in *touch* with their loneliness so he can at least become aware of his condition and understand it as part of being alive.

And now, a final question: Won't the Expectation Buff *always* believe that marriage can cure loneliness as long as two people communicate? He probably will . . . but if he does, he may be in for disappointment. We of THE NATIONAL LOVE, SEX & MARRIAGE TEST believe that nobody can *take care of* another person's loneliness. They can only *care for* it. Realizing the vast difference is nine tenths of this battle *won!*

What Is This Thing Called "Good Communication?"

That's hard to say. I'm still being surprised when, just when I think things are going great, my wife will say, "We haven't been getting along." "We haven't been communicating." And I often find that my take on "communication" and my take on being a "good husband" is quite different from what she thinks I should be doing. At least we will talk about things more now, including dissatisfactions. It doesn't come as quite a shock any more. I have to remember that my criteria for being a good husband and thinking I'm doing all the right things may not be the same as hers, and that I've got to let her know what I want as well.

Anthony Pietropinto, M.D.
New York, New York

People making meaning with each other, and giving each other evidence that they've heard the meaning—that's good communication. For example, when a person wants to ask a question and goes to the other person, gets their attention, and then checks out whether or not they were heard, and the other one does the same.

Dr. Virginia Satir
San Francisco, California

That's a very important question. And this applies to any relationship. I happen to be a very religious person; I'm a Quaker. I think that this opening your-self up to somebody else, to total intimacy, is such dangerous ground for many people that they are al-ways withholding themselves in relationships, even crucial ones, such as in marriage, for instance. We haven't taught our children how to open themselves up to each other in relationships—like between sib-lings, between parents and children—in such a way that they can feel safe and secure and can judge their security and take those steps, to show their vulnera-bilities. We are a suspicious country now. Of every-body, of each other. A very suspicious country. We long for that kind of open relationship. The basis for that is the total security of the mother-child rela-tionship very early in life. And now we are seeing abused and battered children, we are seeing rejected children, we are seeing mothers and fathers who with-hold themselves from each other, and we are becom-ing more and more alienated.

Dr. Mary Calderone
Old Brookville, New York

Well, first of all, I don't see good communication as an end in itself. Communication for me is an instru-mental thing—it is understanding something that you need to understand well enough to move on from there. When things are going well, people are ade-quately communicating. That may need to be very lit-tle—a word, a touch, is all that's needed sometimes. If "I'm doing all the right things and you're doing all the right things and everything's going wrong, so what's happening?" then we have to improve communication.

One of the notions I've been interested in watching is the idea that the more communication, the better. A good marriage questionnaire used to ask, "How *much* do you communicate with your spouse?" Then people thought, well, it wasn't enough that it was "much"—it had to be positive. With negative communication, you could bitch all day and that wasn't good. So then it was how positive is your communication and we measured it on a meter. Then it wasn't enough that it be positive. Before positive, even, it had to be clear-channel communication—like when we had all the electronic models of where the noise entered the system. Then we had whether it's in command form or permissive. Whether the meta-message was something to put you on the defensive in an aggressive or competitive mode, something symmetrical and complementary, something that produced tension, or lateral communication that permitted each person to be equal. Well, that's sort of where we are now, but I've been interested in that simple question about communication.

Unless I know which of these models you're coming from, you could be meaning all different kinds of things, and I would actually reject all of them in the sense that they all tend to set up communication as a goal in itself. It's a process that you go through in order to get combined satisfactions and joint scripts. When you have those, you don't need as much communication and that's why older couples have less of it.

Carlfred B. Broderick, Ph.D.
Los Angeles, California

Why Do Many Couples Have Trouble with Intimacy?

I see a lot of people who will give up on someone who has trouble being intimate because he has difficulty in communicating and relating. They think he can't. Then he doesn't. And then they give up and look for someone from out of the West who will— whom they're not going to find, or he would probably become a bore after several years as well. And lack of communication usually means one of two things. One, "I think I can't communicate well," "I give up," "I evade"; or two, "It's hard to communicate and, therefore, it's too hard," so again, "I give up," and "I don't try." But it can be overcome.

Dr. Albert Ellis
New York, New York

It seems to me that intimacy is the result of trust, of letting a person in, and that the biggest hurdle to intimacy is having been hurt when you let somebody in, or being afraid you'll be hurt. But I don't think anybody's afraid unless they *have* been hurt or unless somebody's filled their ears full of all kinds of stuff. I suppose there are mothers and fathers who train their daughters and sons not to trust the other sex and so on, but my observation is that it's rarely that. It's almost always that somebody's really been screwed over, so in dropping that seventh veil—or even the fifth or the third—it's not a very safe thing to do. They get all uptight and anxious about it. So, to me, intimacy is really opening up to the other person, reciprocally, and it's the product of earned trust (or sometimes un-earned trust, inherited from the romantic fantasy that your mate is perfect and couldn't hurt you).

Carlfred B. Broderick, Ph.D.
Los Angeles, California

That's such a big problem, probably a world-wide problem. I'll tell you what my view of it is. It starts in childhood because people couldn't have intimacy with their own parents. Their own parents didn't show inti-macy to the children and they don't know what inti-macy is. There's a big block of ignorance. That's the biggest thing I've found. The second thing is that many people are afraid they're going to be eaten up by the other person if they interpret intimacy as being willing to give to somebody: "I'll give this and then what will happen? Probably eat me up." The feeling that the other person is going to let you down, the feeling of distrust, and the fear of being made vulnera-ble are very great. But all of this is within the basic framework of that ignorance of what intimacy is re-ally all about. I have what I call my "five freedoms" which define intimacy on a working level: When I can be intimate with you and you with me; when both of us can say what we see and hear instead of "what we should"; when we can ask for what we want instead of waiting for the other one to offer it; when we feel what we feel instead of worrying about whether it's the right feeling; when we take steps in our own be-half instead of always trying to keep the status quo. To me, intimacy is stating all of these as belonging to oneself, belonging to a couple together, owning all of this.

Dr. Virginia Satir
San Francisco, California

What Do You Think
of the Fashionable New Illusion
That Men Should Be Able
to Relate, Communicate, and Feel
the Way Women Do?

I hope it's not a fashion. I think that most men would like to talk and be more nurturing. I think the whole macho trip has largely prevented that. I think this is a sickness in our culture. Frankly, I think it's the woman who can do so much for us. I wrote an article recently for *Ladies' Home Journal* about what women can do for men to make this a better society. For example, with little boys, before they become men, to take the stress away from sports, competitive sports, which I feel are highly destructive. I know I will get a lot of flack on that, but that's how I feel. And I think we got the biggest response of any column I've ever done for the *Journal*. So women certainly went for this position. I think that it's not the woman who has suffered so much to this point—I think it's the man. I think that the man has been ripped off by the culture, that there are all sorts of aspects of himself that he never realized, never developed, never evolved. I think he has a terrible frustration because of these so-called feminine feelings and characteristics, which aren't feminine at all. It's a sick culture that determines what will be "feminine" and what will be "masculine." It destroys so many possibilities and aspects of the average man that were never evolved and will never be developed. The fact that women crave this development in men is a good sign. But they have to do more with a little boy in order to sustain this kind of general cultural development and evolution. If that happens, if mothers become more cognizant of what is important in children of both sexes and that it is just as important for little boys to evolve and develop all of their feelings and yearnings for things artistic, for poetry, what have you, then the chances aren't bad at all. Certainly in the area of sex, it makes for a better lover. The macho man is not a good lover. He has no imagination. He is completely constricted. He has to operate within very well defined boundaries. He's a bore and the average woman knows this. I mean, the average woman who has any kind of contact with the macho man, after the initial attraction—which she is taught to have by society. You can't separate the society from the people who are in it. She is taught to be attracted to a particular man and then is bored silly by him, bored silly by the war stories, the football stories—these are not very interesting to women at all.

Dr. Theodore Isaac Rubin
New York, New York

I hope we move more and more in the direction of men relating to other human beings as women do, more in a personal, caring way. I not only agree with that, I think it is absolutely fundamental to the salvation of our society. It is relating to one another in the traditional male sense of combat and conquest that tears society apart. And, as men, if we care about improving family life and the quality of life in our country, in our world, we have to learn to look at one another as human beings so that we can relate in an affectionate, open way. I don't know whether you have ever noticed or not, but the only time men are viewed on television, or in public, as hugging one another, is after they have scored a goal on a football team, and then the men all race around and they hug each other and embrace, and this is accepted. They have won some type of combat. It seems to me that it is important that we learn to have a touching, caring, open relationship with one another, without having won something in combat first.

Rodney Shaw, Methodist minister
Washington, D.C.

Well, I think there are some qualities that are basically human . . . and they include such things as honor and openness. The great men as well as the great women have these qualities. But I think that the specific sex role, the traditional assignment to women of nurturing and so on, is just as much a cultural phenomenon as the masculine, the macho thing, and I don't see why males *or* females should have to accept that script. It's an application of Rollo May's concept, really—different from the old Puritanism, where you had to be the old way, is the new Puritanism, where you have to be the new way. To depart from the detailed, rigid script, you need to have society's permission. I do not see why a man should have to turn around and be like a woman, very nurturing with the milk of human kindness flowing from both breasts. I would prefer a society, I think, where, although the human virtues would be up there for all to aspire to, individual variations would be tolerated.

Carlfred B. Broderick, Ph.D.
Los Angeles, California

Well, I think if a man can be expressive, and more relating, he is going to have a fuller life. I think a relationship that is based on those principles has got to be more mature, fuller, and more satisfying.

Bernard Berkowitz
New York, New York

I think that men and women need to be liberated in many, many ways, and it seems to me that one of the chief ways that men have needed liberation is in how to get more in touch with their feelings. And one of the problems has been that so many people have only gotten in touch with the anger and not the warm feelings.

Marcia Lasswell
Pomona, California

*What Happens
When Courtship Ends in Marriage?*

The studies that I've done following courtship into marriage find that the courtship is a very good indication of the marriage. For example, if the guy was very excited about the courtship, fell in love early, and virtually seduced his wife into marrying him, a year after they're married he might be thrilled with what he's achieved and happy as a clam, but she's a little less so—just as she was just a little less so during the courtship. The reverse is also true. Where both of them went tripping down the path arm in arm to marriage, a year later both of them are happy. However, in a quarter of the cases where one or the other of them was really reluctant and dragging their feet and got married only because they ran out of alternatives, because of pregnancy, or because life didn't turn out the way they planned it, a year later they're still wondering if they should have done it. They're not too happy. So courtship has proven to be the best single predictor of who will be happy a year later. Even people who have been living together and then get married often find that the very script of marriage itself calls for different behaviors, and so there may be changes. I've known people, for example, who had really great sex lives before they were married but, as soon as they got married, the woman dried up because she was now a married woman like Mamma, and women like Mamma were not sexual cavorters. The husband said, "But what's changed?"

We know that if people get married at the high end of the curve of expectation and enthusiasm, then it seems to be natural for there to be a regression toward the mean, just because it takes so much energy to keep anything at a very high level. I don't care if it's marriage or a teaching career. Let's say the teacher starts out and is going to go out and save the world— ministers do, psychiatrists do, social workers do, nurses do. In any idealistic occupation, including marriage, there is a great deal more enthusiasm at the outset than can be maintained in the natural course of events with competing demands. There are some people who maintain enthusiasm because they have the special skills and interests and energies for it and there are some who find they've been cheated, robbed. The largest group is somewhere in the middle, just sort of getting into a steady kind of pace that lacks the enthusiasm or verve of the beginning of marriage, and yet can be warmly valued.

We are one of the few societies where there's no mechanism for getting people married, except themselves and romantic idealism and so we use that. And because we use it, we have to live with the process of demystification that occurs afterward.

Carlfred B. Broderick, Ph.D
Los Angeles, California

Married couples have to deal with the so-called dirty work in life—hairpins in the sink, dirty socks that haven't been put into the hamper, in general, those parts of ourselves that aren't always attractive. No one can be attractive all the time. In addition, there comes the awareness that there are things that have to be done; and it's like taking two people—each with their own ways of doing things—and focusing on something which has to be done, like handling money, for instance, where there has to be a single way of going. During the romantic period, money is not an issue for many people. Maybe the man is always paying the check. Then, when they get married, how the money is spent and whether or not it is spent for things that each person feels that they need, finding those things that each one needs become the challenge. And so those kinds of things, the everyday things that have to be jointly dealt with, have to be handled by two people. Two energies now have to be blended in such a way that the outcome is acceptable for both. This has the same importance as two nations trying to come together on an issue of some sort. The stakes may sound higher with nations, but I don't think they always are.

Dr. Virginia Satir
San Francisco, California

PART 4 OF THE TEST:
"FEELINGS"

In order to develop true intimacy, partners need to communicate their thoughts, feelings, and emotions to each other.

However, couples often find that interaction with their mates becomes ruled by habit and each may feel emotionally cut off from the other. Or, the search for independence may make it difficult for a person to form a close relationship with another.

Men in particular are taught that to be emotional and openly express one's feelings is a sign of weakness. But revealing one's feelings and emotions, although it may lead to greater personal interdependence, also satisfies many personal needs.

This section of the test will measure how well you are able to express your emotions . . . your *FEELINGS*.

Questions on "Feelings"

QUESTIONS:

Please circle T for those statements you think are true and F for those you think are false.

1. There is no way to know for sure what your mate feels unless they tell you.   (T)   F

2. If people have any pride at all, they're not going to say, "I'm sorry."   T   (F)

3. Crying is a sign of weakness.   T   (F)

4. I often feel embarrassed giving or receiving affection.   T   (F)

5. I would rather say, "I don't want to tell you," than to lie.   (T)   F

SCORING:

For each correct answer, give yourself *10 points*.

MY SCORE FOR "FEELINGS" _____

Please turn the page for the correct answers.

Answers for
Part 4 of the Test: "Feelings"

1. *"There is no way to know for sure what your mate feels unless they tell you."*

   TRUE

   Every person is the only true authority on what he or she is feeling. No one can tell other persons what they are feeling. On the basis of past experience and intimate knowledge, we can make *predictions* about how our mates feel and will behave, but these are probability statements, not foregone conclusions. The way we *think* they feel is not necessarily the way they will feel.

2. *"If people have any pride at all, they're not going to say, 'I'm sorry.'"*

   FALSE

   No one is totally knowledgeable, always in control of situations, or always right. Sometimes we do things we regret later on or we get information which sheds light on some problem situation so that our previous behavior no longer looks appropriate. To apologize, to say, "I'm sorry," shows sensitivity, maturity, and understanding.

3. *"Crying is a sign of weakness."*

   FALSE

   Under emotional stress, crying is a necessary and useful outlet. Too often people suffer from emotional constipation. When they don't know how to express their emotions in socially acceptable ways, they deny that they're having them. Men are usually taught that crying is unmanly. One of the reasons men have a greater number of heart attacks, suffer from more ulcers, and die younger than women may well be that they bottle up their emotions.

4. *"I often feel embarrassed giving or receiving affection."*

   FALSE

   Everyone needs "strokes." Too often we ignore or play down our emotional needs. Giving and receiving affection are important for mental and emotional health. Affection is a special kind of behavior which shows another person that we care about him. Too often a mate may say, "But she knows how I feel about her—why do I have to say it?" We can't read other people's minds and they can't read ours. We need to tell and be told that someone cares.

5. *"I would rather say, 'I don't want to tell you,' than to lie."*

   TRUE

   Honesty is important in intimate relationships. Without openness and honesty, trust cannot develop between two people but, in some situations, being totally open and honest is not the best tactic. Today there is a great emphasis on openness and honesty but these traits may be used as weapons, telling everything even though we know this information will hurt our mates.

SCORING:

Give yourself 10 points for each "False" response to questions 2, 3, and 4. Give yourself 10 points for each "True" response to questions 1 and 5.

EVALUATION:

The higher your score, the more open you are with your feelings and the more sensitive you are to your mate's feelings.

6

EXPECTATION #5:

that changing sex roles will put marriage on self-destruct

This is where the whole discussion of roles comes in. THE NATIONAL LOVE, SEX & MARRIAGE TEST believes that many of the changes in these contracts came into being because of what happened to a lot of suburban women ten or fifteen years ago whose consciousnesses were raised with the arrival of the feminist movement. They had been very well educated but immediately signed on as wives and mothers. When they achieved the house, the second car, and the second child, instead of becoming happier, they became more resentful. Finally they found out why they were so angry. An M.A. changing diapers?

In order to understand the chaotic nature of what's happening to male-female relationships in the United States in this period of change, we should look more to these hidden agreements and what's happened to *them*, thanks to Freidan, Abzug, Steinem, et al.

Before we begin, let us look at the old Archie Bunker "Standard American" type of contract which is untouched by women's lib.

HIS:

I, Jack, stay married to Bessie because she doesn't give me much static about how many hours I spend at work. Be it now forever set forth that I expect Bessie to be totally grateful for my paycheck and responsible for keeping the kids quiet around the house. Sex will be provided whenever I want it (preferably Sunday morning prior to the "NFL Game of the Week" warm-up).

HERS:

I, Bessie, stay married to Jack because my mother told me I'd be lucky to have a husband who didn't chase after other women, come home drunk, or park along the throughway and shoot at the passing muggers. Be it herein noted that I thank God my husband is not one of the sex degenerates I'm always seeing in movies. Jack provides the groceries; I mind the nest, plan the vacations, and decide whose relatives we'll visit when we go back East (or West). Visits to the beauty parlor do not come out of the household budget.

According to the experts, these Standard Americans represent the largest group of American marriages and include most of the solid citizenry who endure life rather than living it. Their roles are equally rigid. This type of secret contract is difficult to renegotiate or change. The reason? For one thing, they rarely go into therapy. Another, and far more important, reason is that there doesn't seem to be much joy in the relationship. What happens when they change and begin to ask themselves whether their life has any meaning? Disappointment and frustration are almost inevitable. Having bought the social formula for what a man and woman should do and be, they share their experience together in mutual resentment.

The sexual part exemplifies the problem in the whole relationship. As we examine the husband's side of it, old Jack is strictly a Saturday-nighter. He does not really care about creating a highly charged, erotic life. On the wife's part, Bessie views sexuality as something to be endured. Have we exaggerated? Slightly. But only to make a point. The Standard American style conforms to the popular notion of what marriage is supposed to be for millions of Americans (why do so many identify with Edith and Archie Bunker?). Communication and societal conditioning over decades is our problem. The marriage participants are out of contact with one another. They, too, are Expectation Buffs. They expected to find their happiness in fitting into the "proper" role of husband or wife, only to discover this happiness becoming more and more meager.

Now let us peruse what we call the "Utopian" or "Mental Health" secret marriage contract, the kind of contract we would be entering into if the changes inspired by the women's movement during the last fifteen years were to become part of our unconscious Expectations. This would be our "official" Utopia:

HIS:

I, Thomas, stay married to Valerie because I can communicate with her as easily as with any male friend—which means that I don't have to patronize her or wonder if I'm going to end up hurting her feelings in some way about something she "doesn't quite understand." Be it also known that I consider our sex life fulfilling because she initiates it at least 50 per cent of the time. In addition, she takes charge of her own needs. She tells me where it feels good *in plain English* and does not hide behind some circumlocutions that came right out of the McGuffey Reader.

HERS:

I, Valerie, stay married to Thomas because I consider him as "aware" and in touch with his feelings (even to crying occasionally) as any of my female friends. May it be further understood that I enjoy sex with him because he seems to be having it *with* me and not turning it into a performance. He's not trying to prove that he's as good as some unknown statistic in the sky. He makes me feel important and sees me as a person. If someone asks Thomas to rate his priorities, I know it would be me first, then the kids, and his career somewhere down the line.

This "Utopian" contract illustrates the kind of marriage that most people in the mental health field queried by THE NATIONAL LOVE, SEX & MARRIAGE TEST consider the ideal, but rarely achieved, marriage contract . . . what we called in the second chapter a "Realistic Romantic" relationship.

This is a mature relationship in which a couple can be straight and direct with each other . . . *real* people who "don't have to play games." On the Freudian model, this is a relationship in which all the Oedipal conflicts and transferences have been "worked through" and where neither partner is using the relationship as a means of re-creating the problems they had with their parents.

As we consider the husband's *realized* Expectations, we see how grateful he is to the mate for taking the initiative in sex a great deal of the time, which shows that the wife is taking responsibility for her own needs, removing a terrific burden from the husband. This indicates a rarely found balance of libidinal needs.

We could not hazard a guess as to how many millions of American couples are living with a great deal of pain because of one mate's turning his body to the other in bed only to find the other not responding. This kind of sexual noncaring is just another example of the "little murders" that cause so much agony in relationships.

The beauty of the "Utopian" marriage is that there are *no* roles to speak of. People are just being nurturing to each other—they just happen to be men and women. Good, fulfilling sex in our "Utopian" contract is but the by-product, the end result, of other, equally important factors in the relationship . . . the foundation upon which everything is built.

The reader should note the high value placed by both Thomas and Valerie on the "friendship," communicating aspects of the relationship. It is obvious that this couple enjoys talking to each other and probably finds each other more interesting than any of their intimate friends. They respect each other's intelligence and enjoy each other's company.

We could hazard a guess that the husband in this kind of

marriage phones the wife spontaneously and asks her out to lunch, preferring her company at times to that of his male companions. Also, he's not too squeamish to take her out for romantic dinners occasionally, buy her "just-because" presents, or spirit her away to some secluded spot in the mountains for an unexpected picnic of wine, cheese, and sex.

Does this mean that the "Utopian" marriage as defined by our experts can only be achieved by people who can spend a lot of time with each other at lunch? Hardly.

Many marriages of this kind can work just as well when the people spend much of their time apart. What we're talking about here is the *quality* of time spent together. The marriage is not seen as a dumping ground for what goes wrong in the outside world.

The reader might observe another salient fact—in our opinion perhaps the most critical one—about this particular couple. Neither his nor her contract mentions anything about inner potential, search for identity, role-playing, or any of the topics one steels himself against when he reads books on relationships which have flooded the market. Each partner accepts the other for what he is, not what he may become according to some rigid model.

And now for the final question: What happens when one partner does change his Expectations? It's simple. After all, we're in Utopia. The *Expectation* is for change. That is the legacy of the women's movement (among others). Let's turn now to our experts for their opinions on changing roles.

*Have Changing Roles for Women
Had a Positive Effect on Marriage?*

We are entering into an age when women and men go into marriage with the idea of it being an equal partnership rather than a dependent, superior/inferior relationship—a partnership in which they will mutually enrich, sustain, and support one another's lives. Part of this, of course, is the trend toward the small family and, in some cases (today, in an increasing number of cases), the child-free family. And this means that the parents are under less financial strain and have more time to spend with each other, to understand and to develop a loving, growing relationship. Part of this, of course, involves responsibility, equal responsibility of the male, for birth control, which is a growing phenomenon in our time. So that when a couple have all the children they want, or as in an increasing number of cases, decide to have no children at all, then the husband takes on the responsibility. He becomes an equal partner in the relationship and he is sterilized, he has a vasectomy. He no longer requires that his wife be in a dependent role, taking the full responsibility.

I think there is more opportunity and more likelihood for romance in terms of an affectionate, caring relationship than there has ever been in the past and that equal roles for women are accepted in our society in an increasing way. Polls indicate that the happiest families as a rule—happiest couples—are those who do not have children. Children do bring strains between husband and wife; and every marriage counselor is acquainted with those strains. These are financial strains; they are strains that come from different ideas of how one disciplines a child, how one raises a child; they are strains of how the attention of the husband or the wife is focused more upon the children than upon the spouse. So I think that probably this trend toward child-free families really is a boost for romance.

Rodney Shaw, Methodist minister
Washington, D.C.

I think that a great deal of it up until recently has had to do with the roles that men had to play as well as the roles that women had to play. I am personally and professionally very enthusiastic about what the women's movement has done in connection with that, because I think for the first time now women are starting to take responsibility for what happens to themselves and are starting to represent themselves in relationships.

Dr. Michael Carrera
New York, New York

I think one of the things that doesn't get mentioned in the unspoken agreement is that the woman is going to take care of the house, she is going to take care of the children if there are any children, she is going to keep the day-to-day things running, the laundry is going to get done by her, the children are going to be sent to school by her. I know that there is a growing feeling among men that they *can* help around the house—it's not just "women's work." But unless this is really spelled out early in the relationship—if you go into marriage with an unwritten contract that says the woman is responsible for this sort of thing—sooner or later there will be dissatisfaction.

One of the other difficulties that I think often comes up—and I think this is implicit in many relationships

—that whither the man goes, the woman goes, and this often gets to be a big problem. Men change jobs but even if the woman is working, too, they just sort of acknowledge that, wherever his job takes him, that's where she's going, too. And I think it's a very difficult thing when a woman tries to change this. In many cases I have seen, the woman actually has the better job, the more promising future. I can think of one—a woman psychiatrist married to a minister— and she said, "Wherever he gets transferred, that's where I have to go." It is just kind of automatically assumed. So that has to be part of a contract, although I don't think many people spell this out to each other. I don't think people say, "When we get married, it's going to be decided that where you go I'm going to go." I think marriages and living-together relationships get into trouble when some of the things which the man assumed were there suddenly get questioned.

Anthony Pietropinto, M.D.
New York, New York

It has produced casualties in some marriages. In any revolution, there are some people who are casualties. For example, in marriages where the husband might have been impotent at, say, forty, he becomes aware of his impotence at a much earlier age . . . let's say, thirty, because he can no longer pretend to himself that he's not having sex because he is respecting his wife, or because he has her feelings in mind. He has to face the fact now that women have sexual needs. Sometimes it panics him at an earlier age.

Dr. Joyce Brothers
Fort Lee, New Jersey

I think that things have become very confusing and I think people have a lot of trouble because what used to be understood sex roles now have to be negotiated. And some people carry it too far. They fight over who makes the dinner on Monday night and, if one person were merely to say, "You do it, because I'm more tired," it could get to be altogether too complicated. I would say that a house needs two captains. People have to define their areas. You can't have two leaders because then you get no leadership in a couple. And I think that somebody finally has to decide something. I don't think it should be decided on the basis of sex— but rather the one who's better at it, for example. I think the only marriage that works nowadays is an equal one.

Dr. William Appleton
Cambridge, Massachusetts

I think that these changes have made it much more difficult to be married. I think that, eventually, it may improve marriage—it may improve relationships and even families—but generally, for the moment, I think that there is much chaos and much difficulty with establishing a new identification for women. And I think men are traumatized to a large degree with the advent of change in women's roles.

Dr. Theodore Isaac Rubin
New York, New York

We now have higher expectations of marriage, and I think that this is why we are seeing a higher divorce rate. On the other hand, we are also seeing a rise in the number of second marriages that do not divorce, that are more successful. I think that, for women, the verbalizations of what one expects from a relationship, and consciousness raising, have been very valuable and I am hoping and thinking that the same kind of process is going to be undertaken by men. They haven't had this opportunity. I have been a professional woman now for a good twenty years. I started very late. I didn't go to work till I was fifty. But, before that, whenever I was out with my husband, I was always put down there with the women while all the men were talking about the things I was interested in. And I finally ended up by going into the men's world, so to speak—joining them there.

Dr. Mary Calderone
Old Brookville, New York

We *have* seen a certain period of transition. Things are changing, and when they change, there is always going to be a certain amount of dislocation. I think that, in the long run, once people are accommodated to things, there will be a greater degree of satisfaction. It's a great relief for many men not to have to be "Big Daddy" all the time. That can make it more comfortable for men in marriage. Once these changes are worked through, marriage can be creatively what any two people want to make it. Women don't have to feel like they are servants, subjugated all the time. I don't know where it's written that it's the woman's responsibility to do the cooking and cleaning. If it's what the two of them think is right, we have the greatest amount of freedom these days to choose and to create life-styles that are satisfying. If that's what you choose, don't feel guilty about it. But if you choose not to be the cook and the cleaner and if the man can take over that role, or part of that role, I say, why not?

People are infinitely different, but the common thread that runs through the fantasies of many people about marriage has to do with finding the ideal person, and that ideal person usually means the super-parent —the one who will always be understanding, loving, giving, who will make everything right and heal all wounds—something that comes from the child's heart and, therefore, has to be an idealized fantasy thing. Usually, if that expectation is too strong and is held on to for too long, it leads to disappointment.

We found a wonderful connection, but I think that Mildred is a wonderful person. She is all that I could ever want her to be. But she's a person, she's not a super-person. And that's the important difference. She has needs. But she's not a dream parent. She's an ideal mate. At times, she's the person to whom I can bring myself when I need some parenting, when I want to be babied; but there are times when it reverses. This is what makes it so wonderful. We're there for each other. When problems really appear in a marriage, it's when the need to be babied collides—he comes home after a hard day's work, and he's just *had it*. And he can't give another thing to another person. She's been home all day, with the kids, the delivery people, and the things going wrong in the chauffering to live in the suburbs, and she can't give another thing to another person. They both need to be given something; they both need to be taken care of. And when those two needs are on a collision course is when you have most of the troubles.

Somebody—and it can't always be the same person —has to have the faith, the trust, and the wherewithal to say, "If I can hold out a little bit longer, I'll get my turn; it will come back to me, if I can just give." And somebody has that little extra bit of endurance, if it's backed up by trust and faith. The important thing is to be there for the other person.

Bernard Berkowitz
New York, New York

The most positive effect I think it's had is that it has made it very clear that women are not just sexual objects, that they're open participants who have the right of scripting themselves. But I think that things have changed, for example, from the days when Albert

Ellis wrote about men finding the "magic button." Women have defined themselves, not merely as sexual objects, but as inputters. And I think that's the most important and valuable cause. I don't think it has been uniformly helpful that women have departed from traditional scripts that men knew what to do with, leaving everybody flailing around, trying to find new scripts. Although it's alerted people to the necessity of negotiating scripts, it has also left many men *and* women without bearing or mooring in terms of knowing their roles. I find that there's a group of women who, thrown into that vacuum, have adopted men's scripts—only to find that, somehow, it hasn't worked out well for them. I think that whenever you disbar a set of scripts—outmode them—you always have flailing around while people try to figure out what *should* now work. That's the handicap of it.

Carlfred B. Broderick, Ph.D.
Los Angeles, California

Well, the divorce rate has gone up, and a lot of people say it's because of women's new freedoms to work and make money and be independent, and so a lot of people would say, "No, that's not very good for marriage." On the other hand, I think what that means is that there are a lot of women who are not staying in unsatisfactory marriages because they can now get out. And so, just because a marriage is stable, it doesn't mean it's a satisfactory marriage. When you say, "Has women's liberation been good for marriages?" it has broken up some that probably were unsatisfactory, but I think for many relationships it has been good—it has changed the way that husbands and wives relate to each other.

Marcia Lasswell, Ph.D.
Pomona, California

PART 5 OF THE TEST:
"ROLES"

The U. S. Census Bureau tells us that, in 1960, 28 per cent of wives with children under eighteen years of age worked. In 1975, 45 per cent (almost half) of these women participated in the labor force.

One still-commonly-held expectation in the United States is that, in a family, the husband is the head of the household and provider of income while the wife is in charge of the day-to-day running of the household and is responsible for the emotional needs of family members. Some people see any deviation from this type of family relationship as harmful both to individual family members and to the family as a whole.

But the United States is going through a period of rapid social change and the structure of the family is changing also. This, our fifth section of the test, will deal with your understanding of *ROLES* in today's family.

Questions on "Roles"

Please circle T for those statements you think are true and F for those you think are false.

1. A woman who works can't be as good a mate as one who doesn't.   T   (F)

2. People are often less satisfied with their marriages if they have children.   T   (F)

3. Men don't like women to take the lead in love-making.   T   (F)

4. If a wife works, the children will have more problems than if she stays at home.   (T)   F

5. It's up to the man to primarily make the basic decisions in a relationship.   T   (F)

SCORING:

For each correct answer, give yourself *10 points*.

MY SCORE FOR "ROLES" _____

Please turn the page for the correct answers.

Answers for
Part 5 of the Test: "Roles"

---

1. *"A woman who works can't be as good a mate as one who doesn't."*

   FALSE

   Research shows that both husbands and wives are lower in tension and higher in sociability if the wife chooses either full-time or especially part-time employ-ment over homemaking. This is less true if the wife feels *forced* to work when she does not wish to and less true when there are preschool children. However, when there are grade-school children, all of the comparisons (for kinds of marriage happiness) favor the labor-market choice.

2. *"People are often less satisfied with their marriages if they have children."*

   TRUE

   Why does the arrival of children result in less marital satisfaction? There are several important reasons. Stud-ies have pointed out that parents receive very little train-ing and preparation for child-rearing. They have little practical experience they can fall back on when the baby arrives. Children make large demands on parents' emo-tional, physical, and financial resources. All too often, taking care of the children leaves little time or energy for spouses to take care of themselves. The marriage relationship is sort of put on the back burner while the kids are at home. A recent study of housewives found that, when asked to rank social roles in their order of importance, women put "mother" first, then "wife."

3. *"Men don't like women to take the lead in love-mak-ing."*

FALSE

Of course, it depends in part on *when* and *how* the "lead" is taken. Most men respond positively to flirtation, subtle hints of sexual availability, and other sexually attractive behavior of women they like if the timing and situation are appropriate. The literature of fantasies certainly indicates that a favored daydream of many men involves encounter with a sexually assertive woman.

"If a wife works, the children will have more problems than if she stays at home."

FALSE

Many horror stories have circulated regarding the effects on the family when mothers work outside the home. Children will be juvenile delinquents. If they manage to escape such a fate, they will grow up emotionally unstable. Husbands can never be happy unless the little woman is at home. Numerous studies have gone a long way in disproving these myths. The mother's absence from home because she was working did not have negative effects on children's personalities. Compared to children whose mothers did not work outside the home, children of working mothers scored the same on power and affiliation measures and even higher when tested for achievement motivation.

"It's up to the man to primarily make the basic decisions in a relationship."

FALSE

Marriages where people are equal when it comes to power decisions, an even division of labor, and high degrees of companionship are healthier than those households which use the one ship/one captain philosophy. So, you men, if you think you should take care of all spending decisions, at least let your wife worry about whether to admit both Red China and Taiwan.

SCORING:

Give yourself 10 points if you answered "True" on

question 2. Give yourself 10 points for each response (
"False" on questions 1, 3, 4, and 5.

EVALUATION:

The higher your score, the more you agree with cu
rent research findings on marriages and other intima
relationships . . . *or* the higher your score, the less yo
rely on "myths" to guide your relationship.

7

EXPECTATION ✳6:

that marriage provides you with built-in emotional security

In our chapter on changing roles, we discussed two kinds of marriages: The first was the Archie Bunker/"Utilitarian" type, and the second was the "Utopian" variety, the kind of marriage where the people involved treat each other as just that—*people*.

For our chapter on trust and freedom, dear readers, we will peruse two other kinds of marriages where these issues seem to be so critical. Thus, as we did in the chapter on roles, let us fling ourselves upon the secret contracts in the "Where Have All the Flowers Gone?" type of marriage.

HIS:

I, Philip, stay married to Debbie because, originally, my parents told me to settle down. I was running around with too many of the wrong kinds of girls. Be it known that I was perfectly aware that the purpose of marriage was to raise kids, establish a career, and get new slippers every third Father's Day, as long as I paid all the bills. What I didn't know was that she'd start calling me "Pops" the minute we brushed the rice off our shoulders—after all, we were both only twenty-three.

HERS:

I, Debbie, stay married to Philip for the purpose of raising geniuses who will get all the advantages we never got when we were kids. Let it be duly noted that I am aware he complains a lot about how much I overinvest in the children and give them top priority, but, actually, dear party of the second part, I don't know another way. Just like Gail Sheehy said in her book *Passages,* I'm too frightened to find out what I want to be when I grow up. From time to time, we take vacations alone so we can recapture the old romance and maybe . . . maybe . . . But I keep thinking the new baby-sitter will burn the house down.

This type of marriage contract, unspoken, of course, i typical of a large segment of American marriages, the kin of couple who were excited by each other at the time thei union was formed but, despite a popular American myt (the pernicious expectation that holds that the advent o children will enrich the marriage), the sex goes *phhfftt* upon the birth of the first child.

Suffice to say that when the first child is brought hom from the hospital, the wife/lover turns into something else She sees herself as a wife/mother. She no longer gets he greatest satisfaction in giving to her husband sexually (th way she thinks society programmed her). Even if sh wanted to, she couldn't. She's worn out from nightly feed ings and emotional pressure caused by the change in he own life.

Meanwhile, our husband sits off in the corner, resentin . . . cut off emotionally and feeling like a second-class citi zen. His needs have become less important. His Expecta tions have been going, going, gone . . . and finally dashed His beloved, the provider of all sexual pleasure, ha recycled herself into something in his wildest dreams h never bargained for when they were shopping for layettes an endlessly tired mother figure.

Now, readers, we're sure you're probably aware that th "Where Have All the Flowers Gone?" child-centere ouples represent a very large segment of American marriages. Being Expectation Buffs and hopeless Romantics, ou should now be asking, "What keeps these marriages oing?"

The husband stays with the relationship because he's omfortable, society expects it, he's afraid of what's outside and facing loneliness, and he feels too guilty about eaving the children. He's a prisoner. From time to time, he might take a trip out of town and indulge in a brief ling or a one-night stand. These are fine old American ustoms sanctioned by our double standard of sexual conluct (a standard increasingly less acceptable these days).

What about the wife? Once she has a child, an identity comes with the territory. She can fill the role of mother vell into middle age. Curiously, however, as we pointed out in our chapter on roles, the wife may be just as miserable in the contemporary middle-class marriage as her complaining husband. She's programmed to be happy and can't figure out why she isn't.

The chief saving grace for this couple is that *they are both keenly aware something is missing:* the mutuality and caring they shared prior to the birth of the first child. They have something very real in the history of their relationship and could renegotiate their contract if they wanted to become aware that there was a contract. The question is: Do they want to go through the real pain of doing it?

Now let us peruse our second kind of marriage, the kind of marriage where people refuse to *really* renegotiate their total contract but choose to change one facet of it, to focus primarily on the sexual provisions of their contract. Let's delve into the "Open Marriage" contract:

HIS:

I, Frank, stay married to Carla because I believe that the freedom and separateness I want for myself should be harnessed to the freedom and separateness she wants for herself (but I want just a little more for me). Using this as a general proposition, there shall be no such thing as jealousy, possessiveness, or "cheating," since I will come home and honestly discuss such "cheating" freely and openly. Naturally, since she is a rational person, I hope she'll do the same so I won't feel overly guilty.

HERS:

I, Carla, stay married to Frank because he says if I don't give him the freedom to experiment with other women, he'll leave me. Let it be duly noted that I wish we could cease and desist from all those group sex and swap club events he's always trying to get me to go to, because I don't want to be offered up like a sacrifice. Sometimes I think if only I were more open and supportive of him, he wouldn't feel the need for other women, but if I tell him I think he's terrific, he might feel confident enough to leave me.

This type of secret contract, gentle reader, was expose a few years ago when the book *Open Marriage* became s popular. Many couples were engaged in extramarital affairs anyway, but could now find sanctions for what the were doing. Others were going through the first head moves of radical feminism, breaking down old values, an seeking new cultural mores.

What their not-*that*-secret contract confirmed for eac other is that they are not possessive of each other, tha they are expected to squelch jealousy, and that they ar both perfectly capable of dealing with a primary marita relationship and an infinite number of nonprimary sexua liaisons. They maintain that one can be close and sexuall intimate with other people without endangering one's mar riage. Certainly, there is much in the current popular an psychological literature to support their views. According to many books of the early seventies, this kind of rela tionship is ideal . . . a marriage in which two people ar self-contained, self-actualized, and self-satisfied. According to this thesis, once the couple has established their separat identities, it is possible, even desirable, to handle mor than one sexual relationship.

First, let's look at the positive aspects of these "open

ended" marriages. They get points from us for at least
questioning and discussing the basic nature of their relationships in order to realize that, at least on some level,
they have to *negotiate* change. The marriage is not something that's stuck up on the wall like Uncle Herbert's
moose.

At least one of the partners has risked coming to grips
with his expectations (the conscious parts) and has had to
negotiate for a change. The couple creates another type of
marriage contract, albeit a highly volatile, often destructive
one. Frank and Carla seek some intensity, excitement,
and romance out of their day-to-day existence.

The down side of the Open Marriage contract? According to our experts, as we shall soon see, very few of them
seem to think open marriage works. In practice, many
couples involved in open marriage seem to be of a particular breed. At least one partner seems to be cut off, rigid,
not comfortable with feelings, and with a limited tolerance
for closeness in a one-to-one relationship. The couple may
be involved with each other, but whatever intensity exists
has to be structured and constantly worked at—in many
cases by group sex, swap clubs, nudist colonies, encounter growth groups, etc., etc.

What does the cut-off spouse get out of this arrange-
ment? The cut-off partner makes a particular kind of
trade-off. If the spouse can go out and satisfy the need for
intimacy elsewhere, the other partner can do the same.
Since they're being good sports about it and it is all open
and agreed to formally, there should be no guilt or jealousy and few complaints.

It is the opinion of THE NATIONAL LOVE, SEX & MAR-
RIAGE TEST, however, that both are being shortchanged.
Once there may have been an effort to get pleasure in a
marriage—intimacy and closeness from each other—but
the effort usually deteriorates when either person gets close
to others. Many destructive things happen. When both
people are equally involved with outside relationships,
things appear to go smoothly. However, when one of the
outside relationships ends and the spouse is still involved in
a relationship, there is usually much resentment, anger, and

feelings of abandonment which could ultimately ruin the marriage.

The paradoxical problem in both the marriages we have just looked at is that both couples sign an unconscious contract they cannot keep. Both were unaware of an even deeper, far-more-secret Expectation—a basic Expectation, all pervasive Expectation, that we require from any marriage worthy of the name.

What is it? That each married the other to feel good in this world and that both could provide enough security to the other person so they wouldn't have to go to other people for it. This is the basic contract that underlies the whole issue of freedom and, more important, trust. And now, on to our experts' comments on this subject.

Can Open Marriage Work?

Generally speaking, the idea of open marriage works splendidly in a book. In our culture, it does not seem to work very well. The couples who have followed open marriage seem to believe that they are improving their marriage right up to the time that they pack their bags and leave for Reno. And in cultures where people are brought up to feel that you can have several relationships—i.e., there are places today where a woman can legally have several husbands at the same time, where one husband is the "fix-it husband," fixing things around the house; there is the "worker husband," who goes out and works in the field; and the third is the "lover husband." And, for that culture, that works very well. But in our culture, where we vow fidelity and we believe that there should be a one-to-one relationship, the idea of open marriage just doesn't seem to work out. If you don't care about the other person emotionally, then sex with that person is about as satisfying as a sneeze. If you do care about the other person emotionally, it interferes with the primary relationship of the marriage.

Dr. Joyce Brothers
Fort Lee, New Jersey

I think they have been an abysmal failure, because people just didn't want them. The fact is that most people still want exclusive relationships and really feel terribly threatened by the possibility of relationships that are otherwise. The rational emotive therapy—it doesn't work. The fact is that these open marriages aren't successful.

Dr. Theodore Isaac Rubin
New York, New York

Well, I have a good opinion. I wrote a book called *The Civilized Couple's Guide to Extra-Marital Adventure,* which shows a lot of sexual aspects and also how to be unjealous and how to have an open marriage. But I still think that most people won't go through RET—rational emotive therapy—to prepare themselves for the ideal—and it is an ideal—where I am married to one and it's a one-to-one loving relationship and I also allow myself and she allows me to have other, open relationships on the side.

Dr. Albert Ellis
New York, New York

Well, I have never seen it work. I have looked, but have never seen an open marriage. I've read about it, but I've never seen it. I feel that *three* cannot make a marriage, but maybe I don't know about it.

Dr. Virginia Satir
San Francisco, California

I think it's a noble idea, the idea of the lack of possessiveness and so on. But by being fully in touch with people's need for variety, growth, and freedom and those good things, open marriage totally overlooks and underestimates the need people have for security, for stability, for possessiveness. And I think it turns out to be a contradiction. About two or three years ago, I had a rash of people falling out of their open marriages and feeling very guilty. They said, "Where am I failing? I really believe in this. My head's really in this place, so why am I jealous, why is this?" In effect, I think it calls for a level of personal morality and sacrifice that's saintlike, and it's not too surprising to me that very few humans would achieve it. I have not really seen any that worked, although I would not deny that there might be some. But, then, I tend to run in circles where either they wouldn't do it or, if they do do it, the reason I see them is because they're clients.

Carlfred B. Broderick, Ph.D.
Los Angeles, California

I was talking to another analyst the other day who said that most of her patients seem to have multiple relationships, whereas the people I work with occasionally do have other relationships than the serious relationship they are in, but mostly they are interested in a one-to-one relationship. I think we are coming back to that. I would say ten years ago there were more affairs going on. People have kind of come back from that. Even the O'Neills. I know Mrs. O'Neill has written a book in which she talks about the one-to-one relationship. And that's a far cry from her open marriage.

Mildred Newman
New York, New York

I have feelings about it and I always have had. I have always had suspicions of it. Now my suspicions are being confirmed by the marriage counselors, including the O'Neills, who coined that phrase. And what are my suspicions? Well, it's the rare marriage that can stand totally open marriage constantly. And now we are assuming—experts have said it, sex therapists have said it—that it's really only about 10 per cent of marriages that can really withstand extramarital sexuality.

Dr. Mary Calderone
Old Brookville, New York

How Much Do People Have to Give Up to "Make a Go of It"?

I don't think I have given any of myself up. What has happened is that we have both grown to be more fulfilled people, better people, more interesting people, because he brings to me all the things that I would never notice in the world, or be excited about, and I feel that I have done the same for him. So rather than losing anything, I feel that we have both gained. It's a gestalt, it's more than just the sum of our parts. Yes, we have other interests, and we have our own excitement in terms of the things we like to do—for example, my husband enjoys watching television and the sports on television. In fact, if we were ever to get a divorce—which we never plan—the only way he would know it is if they announced it on "Wide World of Sports." And, for me, that is a boring thing to do. So my interests lie elsewhere, and he does not share in those, but we are certain to have mutual interests. We've bought a farm, and being city people—born in New York City, brought up in New York City—I thought that cows slept on their backs at night so the cream would be on top in the morning, and we are learning about farming and that is our mutual interest.

Dr. Joyce Brothers
Fort Lee, New Jersey

Not enough. If they wanted to make a good relationship, they would give up a good part of their desire, because there are conflicting desires in a good relationship but they wouldn't give up themselves in the sense of doubting themselves, or giving up by berating themselves, or by doubting the other human being . . . so they don't give up enough of their desire, and give up too much of themselves, meaning that they put themselves down if they don't act well, beautifully, etc.

Dr. Albert Ellis
New York, New York

I have a little diagram that I use to talk about this. For everything we pay a price. The question is, "What are my priorities?" If I'm eating too much, I pay the price of giving up my wish to be skinny. But if I give up all my eating, I die—some people do that, too. So you've got two people who want to get married. They are going to have a relationship There has to be an overlap, there has to be enough there for each person so that he or she can continue to be a person, moving around in their own center, but enough there so that they share a center as well. If it develops that one of these people has to give up more than what they keep, they've lost their personhood. Now, just how wide this overlap needs to be depends on the resilience and broadness of each of these people, and people work that out in a variety of ways, ways that are right for both of them.

Dr. Virginia Satir
San Francisco, California

Well, I think you have to be willing to give up a little something to get sometimes a lot more back. And I think this is the problem—people aren't willing to give up. They don't want to give anything up of themselves. There is too much of this selfishness now. The individual is suddenly more important than the partnership. Our partnership has been more important really than us as individuals in our marriage.

Jane Appleton
Cambridge, Massachusetts

Women, more so than men. Very often we will see in therapy, especially women who are in their mid-forties, children who are virtually all grown-up, going to college, leaving home, they'll talk in terms of "what they did" before they were married, the promises they might have had, what they might have had, what they might have achieved if they had gone on their own. I think it's particularly upsetting now, when there is so much more emphasis, so much more acceptance in society about women having careers, women achieving things on their own. And they do often look back at this with a lot of regret. Another thing that often happens is that men in the twenty- or thirty-age range—they are doing a lot of changing, a lot of career evaluation, and the wife is often just kind of trotting along, and sort of defers her own gratification. We are acknowledging more and more in psychiatry that people change. Sigmund Freud somehow gave us the idea that you made it through adolescence and you were nice and healthy and you were going to be fine from then on. You had negotiated the straits and you could then go on to clear sailing. You were a mature individual. People keep changing constantly, and this is something you have to warn your children about. You are going to change during that marriage or that relationship. You had better be aware of what's going on and keep evaluating yourself, but that's a problem, too.

Anthony Pietropinto, M.D.
New York, New York

I think we have had the myth that we must give up our freedom in marriage. Indeed, people give up a great deal of their freedom. I don't think we necessarily have to give up as much freedom as we have in certain models of marriage, but, clearly, there is no such thing as total freedom in any relationship; even if it's with your pet, your dog—you've got to go home and feed him. So you never have total freedom. You always give up some freedom in a relationship.

Marcia Lasswell, Ph.D.
Pomona, California

What Are the Hazards
of an "Unspoken" Contract?

The expectation that another person will make you happy is very great in this country. In the movies it was too romantic, and now we've gone from one extreme to another. We had very romantic 1930s movie marriages where everybody's happy and now, suddenly, people have awakened and become, I think, too cynical, so that nobody's happy. I think someday we are going to come back to the middle of the pendulum swing. We won't expect the moon, we will expect something realistic—and then we won't have to break up our marriages. I think that people who have broken up their marriages—according to feedback that's coming in three, five, or ten years later—are not always so happy about it. It's like any experiment—people are reporting back. They feel, I think, disrupted. I don't think that *all* marriages should stay together but I'm sure there are many that should. I really think people ought to have very serious thoughts before they divorce because they could be hurting themselves.

Jane and Dr. William Appleton
Cambridge, Massachusetts

There are basically two hazardous unspoken "contracts": There is the "I want you to do what I want you to do, and if you don't do it, you're dead," and the "I'm nothing and you make me everything and, without you, your approval, or your energy, I'm nothing." I see it as a horrendous scramble for some sense of self. It's a very interesting thing, because on the principle of "you make me happy," so to speak, the "you" becomes a substitute for "me." And, of course, if you go on doing it, I soon become a burden to you. And yet it's very easy to see how this comes about between couples, because this is usually what the parent-child thing is. Mamma smiles and she says, "You've made me smile." So Mamma *couldn't* smile for any other reason.

Dr. Virginia Satir
San Francisco, California

Myself, I am against any kind of contract. I think the contract we ought to make more is one of spontaneity. And let's see where it goes. The relationship isn't established the moment that we meet and decide to have a relationship. As a matter of fact, the word ought to be obliterated entirely. There is a relating process that takes place, but it's not there until it's there. So you and I, if we have a relationship, have to evolve out that relating, and see where it goes, and how it goes. If we pin ourselves down to any kind of contract, then we are already planting the seeds of ruination because there is something very stagnating about contracts. We are putting it on a business basis, and it is not an economic business affair.

The unspoken contract is really one based on all kinds of claims, with the expectation of instant understanding, instant fulfillment on all bases, instant involvement, sustained interest on the most heightened basis possible, and this, of course, is impossible. This is not within the possibility of the human condition.

Dr. Theodore Isaac Rubin
New York, New York

PART 6 OF THE TEST:
"TRUST"

Without a feeling of trust in one's partner, true intimacy is not possible. To develop a sense of trust in one's mate requires sharing of feelings, mutual caring, and self-disclosure on the part of both mates.

Trust and freedom are interlocked. The more you can depend on your partner, the more freedom you have and the less you need to control your partner.

But some people are unwilling to put too much trust in their partner, since trust in another makes people vulnerable to disappointment and hurt.

In this final section of the test, you will find just how *TRUSTING* and free a relationship you and your partner have.

Questions on "Trust"

QUESTIONS:

Please circle the letter of the answer you think is correct.

1. The partners who have the most freedom in their relationships are those:
    A) who live together without being married.
    B) who respect the rights (freedom and privacy) of their partner.
    C) who are financially successful.

2. If two people trust each other, it's okay to:
    A) open each other's mail.
    B) listen in on the phone, but not open the other's mail.
    C) discuss what kind of privacy they want.

3. At a party, if an attractive person of the opposite sex pays a lot of attention to my mate, I would:
    A) have confidence in my mate.
    B) try to attract someone else, too.
    C) try to conceal my feelings.

4. If I discovered my mate had an affair with someone else, I would:
    A) know my mate didn't love me any more.
    B) have an affair myself.
    C) talk about it, and work things out.

5. If my mate has a hobby that I don't care for, it is best:
    A) to do it, too, even if I don't like it.

    B) for my mate to do something else we both can enjoy.

    C) for each of us to give in a little.

SCORING:

For each correct answer, give yourself *10 points*.

MY SCORE FOR "TRUST" _____

Please turn the page for the correct answers.

Answers for
Part 6 of the Test: "Trust"

---

1. *"The partners who have the most freedom in their relationship are those:*
   A) who live together without being married.
   B) who respect the rights (freedom and privacy) of their partner.
   C) who are financially successful."

The Correct Answer Is: (B)

Freedom cannot be measured objectively. No adult has the inherent right to control another, married or not. What constitutes restraints in one relationship may not in another. It's how the two people define the relationship that determines how free each of the partners is. Each couple must define (decide) on what types of freedoms they desire and will accept.

2. *"If two people trust each other, it's okay to:*
   A) open each other's mail.
   B) listen in on the phone, but not open the other's mail.
   C) discuss what kind of privacy they want."

The Correct Answer Is: (C)

A person cannot *assume* that some act is acceptable to one's partner without "checking it out." Just because Ma and Pa did it this way doesn't mean it's going to work in your relationship. Again, communication, discussion, and a willingness to compromise are the bases for an intimate, loving relationship.

3. *"At a party, if an attractive person of the opposite sex pays a lot of attention to my mate. I would:*
   A) have confidence in my mate.
   B) try to attract someone else, too.
   C) try to conceal my feelings."

The Correct Answer Is: (A)

Trying to "get even" with a partner for behavior of which you do not approve rarely does anything other than escalate the hostility of the other persons involved. On the other hand, trying to conceal one's true feelings is not usually productive behavior, either. Having feelings is always all right. People get into trouble, however, for handling their feelings through ineffective *behavior*. If you answered that you would have confidence in your mate, you are probably better as a partner.

4. *"If I discovered my mate had an affair with someone else, I would:*
   A) know my mate didn't love me any more.
   B) have an affair myself.
   C) talk about it, and work things out."

The Correct Answer Is: (C)

No matter how painful it may seem, trying to work things out is a better solution than jumping to the conclusion that your mate doesn't love you . . . and certainly better than retaliation by having an affair, too. In fact, if one wishes to hold a relationship together, the latter is unfair to the object of the affair, too.

5. *"If my mate has a hobby that I don't care for, it is best:*
   A) to do it, too, even if I don't like it.
   B) for my mate to do something else we both can enjoy.
   C) for each of us to give a little."

The Correct Answer Is: (C)

Even if it is not the ideal solution for either person, a compromise that works is better than having a "winner" and a "loser," even over what to do with leisure time. Demanding that a partner do something you both enjoy when the hobby is a true pleasure is likely to result in resentment whether it is expressed or not (better get a hobby of your own!).

SCORING:

If you circled "A" for question 3, give yourself 10 points, and give yourself another 10 points if you answered "B" to question 1. Give yourself 10 points for each "C" response to questions 2, 4, and 5.

EVALUATION:

The higher your score, the less you need to control your mate's life and the more freedom you have in your relationships.

"How Good a Mate Are You?"

TOTAL TEST SCORES
AND EVALUATION

When dealing with human behavior and emotions, predictions about how an individual will act cannot be 100 per cent certain. Rather, predictions are based on probability statements. That is, if we make predictions about a group of people, our predictions may not hold for all the people in that group. For people who make a perfect score on THE NATIONAL LOVE, SEX & MARRIAGE TEST, we would predict that, on the basis of their scores, they *probably* would be good mates. The odds are in favor of those people being better partners than those whose scores are very low. In turn, if an individual has a low score on the test, it does not automatically mean that he or she is a poor partner.

Although people get a score for each question in this test, whether they get a correct or incorrect answer to a *given* question is not the best predictor of how good a relationship they have nor how good a mate they are. It is more important to look at the over-all score for *each section* and for the *test as a whole*. Some people may score very high on five out of the six sections but do very poorly in one section. Others may miss a few questions in all the sections.

In general, the answers to the questions are based on research findings on intimate relationships and interpersonal communication. But no rule about human behavior holds true for all people and all relationships. As you have seen, the experts have modified some of the answers in their comments and these answers to the test questions can be used as a general guideline to evaluate you, your partner, and your relationship together.

"HOW GOOD A MATE ARE YOU?"
(TOTAL TEST SCORES AND EVALUATION)

Fill in the spaces below with your scores from each section of the test, then total the entire column.

TEST ON "LOVE" . . . . _____

TEST ON "SEX" . . . . _____

TEST ON "ROLES" . . . . _____

TEST ON "FIGHTING" . . . . . _____

TEST ON "FEELINGS" . . . . . _____

TEST ON "TRUST" . . . . _____

TOTAL TEST SCORE: _____

HOW DO YOU COMPARE WITH THE NATIONAL SAMPLE?

If your score was 210 points, you did better than 30 per cent of the national sample. If you scored 230 points, you had a higher score than half of our sampling. If your score was 250 points, you did better than 70 per cent of the people polled across the country, and if you got just one additional question correct, giving you 260 points, you outscored 90 per cent of the sample. Did you score 290 or above? Congratulations! You bettered *99 per cent* of the entire national sample!

8

SPECIAL BONUS TEST:

"are you as sexual and/or as sensual as you think you are?"

This test is *not* part of the NBC television "Big Event," "The National Love, Sex & Marriage Test." It was created especially for you who have purchased the book by Carly Buchanan, Ph.D., a specialist in sex education, and sexual therapists Eleanor Katzman, M.A., M.F.C., and Sam Katzman, M.A., M.S., of Los Angeles.

You *can* take the test by yourself but, hopefully, you will take it with your sex partner to receive its maximum benefits.

Feelings About Sexuality in General

Men and women are raised in separate, sexual worlds which lead to a false set of expectations for both: Men are encouraged to be sexually active (as proof of their "manhood") but to repress tenderness, gentleness, and nonsexual emotions generally, since these are "feminine" qualities. Women, on the other hand, are encouraged to express their emotions generally, except for those that threaten a man's sense of "masculinity," such as being aggressive or taking the initiative sexually. The result is that, when men "reach" for their partners, "it doesn't *feel* like love" to women, who want a demonstration of *non-sexual* affection first, in order to be convinced that the man "really cares." To most men, this is incomprehensible, since they were raised to repress those feelings in all areas *except* sex. And so, while the "sexual revolution" may have changed the behavior of millions of Americans (who now have a wider variety of activities in their sexual gamut), in many cases it has *not* changed the way people *feel* about what they are doing, or failing to do.

If your pencils are ready, let's begin with the first section of the test: "Feelings About Sexuality in General" (before we get into sensuality).

SECTION #1:

Test on
"Feelings About Sexuality in General"

	HIS ANSWER	HER ANSWER
1. Do you consider female sexuality a response to male sexuality—or is it something women control themselves?		
A) Primarily a response to the male partner's need.	———	———

B) Women should control their
sexuality. _____ ✓_____

2. Do you feel that female sexuality
has a complex nature of its own,
or is it pretty much the counterpart of what you consider male
sexuality to be?

A) Female sexuality is complex
and different. _____ ✓_____

B) Female sexuality is the same
as male sexuality. _____ _____

3. When you are making love to your
partner, what kind of feeling do
you experience when your partner
does not have an orgasm?

A) I become sad. ✓_____ _____

B) I feel it's okay and that it's
only one incident out of
many . . . better luck next
time. _____ ✓_____

C) I feel there's something
wrong with me. ✓_____ _____

D) I feel there's something
wrong with my partner. _____ _____

4. In making love, what do you
usually do if your partner does
not have an orgasm?

A) Reassure my partner and
go to sleep. _____ _____

	HIS ANSWER	HER ANSWER

B) Ask my partner if there's something I'm doing wrong, but try to get the anxiety out of my voice. _____ _____

C) Find out if there's something my partner would like from me to add to his/her pleasure. _____ _____

Sexual Communication

Men were supposed to be "strong and silent" (like John Wayne), women were permitted to cry (a sign of "weakness" equated with "feminity") but not to get angry ("too aggressive"), and *nobody* was supposed to say, "I want . . ." ("too selfish"). No wonder we all grew up unable to communicate! And nowhere is communication more difficult than in the area of sex: too little factual information, too many taboos, a plethora of "how-to" manuals dealing with sexual positions, and a real dearth of training on how to *talk to* a partner about one's likes and dislikes. Some people resort to nonverbal messages (leaving a book on the table, hoping it will be read); others use generalized statements like, "They say . . ."

SECTION #2:

Test on "Sexual Communication"

	HIS ANSWER	HER ANSWER
1. Can you communicate your sexual needs to your partner by requesting those specific sexual techniques you prefer?		

	HIS ANSWER	HER ANSWER

A) No, I like things to happen spontaneously. _____ _____

B) I'm usually too embarrassed to ask. _____ _____

C) Yes, I'm very open about it. _____ _____

2. If your partner does not indicate specific sexual needs to you:

A) I ask what my partner would like. _____ _____

B) I explore physically to discover what *exactly* is pleasing. _____ _____

C) I assume the partner is fulfilled. _____ _____

3. Does it make you uncomfortable when your partner requests special sexual techniques as stimulation?

A) No, it excites me to fulfill my partner's sexual request. _____ _____

B) I like to do it only if it's something with which I'm comfortable. _____ _____

C) As long as it's the missionary position, I'll do it. _____ _____

	HIS ANSWER	HER ANSWER

4. Do you find it easy to respond verbally as well as physically to the verbal requests of your partner during love-making?

    A) No. Having to answer back interrupts my concentration.   _____   _____

    B) I respond verbally because it pleases my partner, but I don't like it much.   _____   _____

    C) Yes. Anything that pleases my partner pleases me.   _____   _____

5. If your partner asks you what you especially enjoy, sexually, do you find it easy to specify these things?

    A) No, I like to be surprised.   _____   _____

    B) Yes. I believe in honest communication.   _____   _____

    C) I think asking takes the romance out of it.   _____   _____

6. During love-making, do you talk to your partner, making the partner aware that what's being done is pleasing, especially stimulating, or uncomfortable to you?

    A) I only tell the partner when it's pleasing. I'm afraid I'll hurt the partner's feelings if

	HIS ANSWER	HER ANSWER

what's being done makes
me uncomfortable.

B) I never tell the partner during . . . but when I get up
in the morning, I might
leave a note on the night
stand.

C) You bet!

7. Are you aware of or do you respond to the specific murmurs,
sounds, and words that your partner makes during love-making?

A) My partner never does any
of these things during love-
making.

B) Yes, I know when I'm satisfying my mate.

C) No, it might embarrass the
partner if I acknowledge
anything like noises and/or
murmurs.

8. Do you prefer that your partner
respond to the specific sounds,
murmurs, etc., that *you* make
during love-making?

A) No. It embarrasses me and
makes me quiet.

B) Yes . . . it shows acknowl-
edgment.

Touching

One of the best ways of meeting the body's sensory needs is through stroking and loving touching. It is a way of sensitively "tuning in" to another person, a form of building trust, and the key experience that takes people away from philosophical living and gets them in touch with themselves and each other. Being held and cuddled plays an important role in a child's emotional growth, and it is a need that persists throughout adult life. Yet, in this country, the taboos against touching one another are enormous: Where Italians and French touch each other a hundred times an hour during conversation, Americans make contact fewer than three! We sit or stand near one another in buses, elevators, and movie theaters, and are so terrified of being touched that accidental contacts result in embarrassed apologies and eyes firmly fixed on the floor or the ceiling.

SECTION ⚹3:

Test on "Touching"

	HIS ANSWER	HER ANSWER
1. When you are with your partner (before making love), do you		

	HIS ANSWER	HER ANSWER

caress, touch, fondle, hug, and kiss each other?

A) Seldom. _____ _____

B) Often. _____ _____

C) A great deal. _____ _____

D) Never . . . unless my football team has just scored a touchdown. _____ _____

2. In relationships and love-making, do you feel that touching is:

A) Insignificant. _____ _____

B) All right once in a while. _____ _____

C) Somewhat important. _____ _____

D) Very important. _____ _____

3. Do you enjoy your partner touching and exploring your body to find your especially sensitive and sensually responsive areas?

A) It's the greatest pleasure in sex. _____ _____

B) No, I am shy about revealing my body. _____ _____

4. Do you thoroughly explore your partner's body with your hands,

HIS HER
ANSWER ANSWER

lips, or tongue to determine their
most responsive and sensual areas?

A) Yes, if I'm not tired. _____ _____

B) Yes, but only if I'm feeling
especially loving. _____ _____

C) No, that kind of thing
makes me nervous. _____ _____

D) Absolutely! _____ _____

5. If your partner is shy about touching your body or his/her own,
do you take the lead and guide
your partner's hands to the various areas of your body as well as
your partner's?

A) No. I'm afraid my partner
will think I'm displeased. _____ _____

B) Yes, but only the first time.
After that, my partner's on
his/her own. _____ _____

C) Yes, a few times gently until my partner understands
my needs. _____ _____

6. Do you engage in massage during
love-making?

A) Definitely. It's more relaxing
than a week in the coun-
try. _____ _____

	HIS ANSWER	HER ANSWER
B) No . . . it messes up our quilted bedspread.	_____	_____
C) What's massage?	_____	_____

Fragrances

(BATHING AND SHOWERING; BODY ODORS)

Since one of our most primitive senses is our sense of smell, odors play an important role in our reaction to people and situations. Just as the smell of food can whet our appetite or kill it, body odors can have the same effect on romance. Because we are constantly subjected to advertising for soaps, sprays, and deodorants, we have built up an aversion to natural body odors, and bathe more frequently than most people on this planet. We have "learned" that all personal odors are disagreeable and should be eliminated, hidden, or covered. Actually many people find that natural body odors, especially in a cherished partner, are highly exciting and erotic.

SECTION ※4:

Test on "Fragrances"

	HIS ANSWER	HER ANSWER
1. Do you notice when your partner uses a different perfume, fragrance, cologne, or body oil?		

	HIS ANSWER	HER ANSWER

A) Yes, but only if I bought it for my partner. _____ _____

B) Yes, I'm aware of fragrances and notice new ones. _____ _____

C) No, I never notice. _____ _____

2. Can you name at least one or two of your partner's favorite fragrances?

   A) No, but I'm aware of differences. _____ _____

   B) No, they're all great. _____ _____

   C) My partner doesn't have a favorite fragrance. _____ _____

3. Do you especially like the natural body odor or fragrance of your partner just after the partner has bathed (that is, squeaky-clean before any lotions or perfumes are applied)?

   A) Yes, I'm the naked type. I like the odor of a clean body. _____ _____

   B) I can take it or leave it. _____ _____

   C) Never notice it. _____ _____

4. Do you often find perspiring bodies (yours and your partner's)

	HIS ANSWER	HER ANSWER

pleasant to your senses or stimulating to you sexually?

    A) Yes, I do.

    B) No, I abhor them.

5. After making love, do you usually find your combined body odor:

    A) titillating?

    B) nonexistent (I'm not aware of any)?

    C) definitely unpleasant?

6. Do you and your partner shower or bathe together—washing, caressing, and fondling each other?

    A) Of course—there's an energy crisis.

    B) Frequently.

    C) Never.

7. Do you occasionally shower or bathe with your partner as a lead-in to making love?

    A) Yes, bathing and showering together creates a feeling of caring and togetherness.

    B) Never. Have you seen our water bill lately?

Disrobing

Fantasy plays an important part in most sexual relationships and what people do in getting undressed can provide great stimulation. Gypsy Rose Lee excited a few generations of men by making disrobing an art, and while most women are not professional stripteasers, every woman's body is a source of pleasure to the person who loves her. In addition, most *women's* fantasies include being undressed, slowly and admiringly, by someone they love. Men enjoy it too.

SECTION ⌗5:

Test on "Disrobing"

	HIS ANSWER	HER ANSWER
1. In removing your clothes before making love, do you and your partner prefer to:		
A) take each other's clothing off?	_____	_____
B) watch each other disrobe?	_____	_____

C) get your clothes off as quickly and efficiently as possible? _____ _____

D) undress in private? _____ _____

Do you find it enjoyable (or more thrilling) to make love with some lighting (be it soft lighting, candlelight, daylight, etc.)?

A) No, I feel embarrassed being stared at. _____ _____

B) I love any light as long as it doesn't come from the television set. _____ _____

C) Yes, soft indirect lighting is romantic. _____ _____

Do you feel comfortable while your partner explores your body visually?

A) Yes, I like to be admired. _____ _____

B) No. I'm shy. _____ _____

C) Yes, I get pleasure by watching my partner's response to seeing my body. I also get excited by seeing my partner's body. _____ _____

CHECK YOUR ANSWERS

"Sexuality in General"

1. *The correct answer is:* (B)

Viewing female sexuality as a response to male se:
uality leads to the acceptance of a practice which
probably the greatest single deterrent to sexual enjo
ment, namely the idea that, when a man has an ere
tion, his partner has an obligation. The very same ma
who wouldn't dream of insisting that his partner e:
because *he* is hungry will think nothing of demandir
sex because he is "horny."

2. *The correct answer is:* (A)

The focus of a *man's* sexuality tends to be on th
penis and it is probably because female sexuality wa
thought to be the counterpart of male sexuality that s
much emphasis has been placed on intercourse an
not enough on foreplay. Women's sexuality is differe:
from men's, but they both require patience and atte:
tion.

3. *The correct answers are:* (A) *and* (C)

Raised on the idea that a skillful lover can "give
his partner an orgasm, both partners feel cheate
when *one* doesn't climax. To him, either she is frigi
or worse yet, he is inadequate; to her, it proves he
selfish and inconsiderate and only interested in h
own sexual release. When it's the *man* who doesn
reach orgasm, his first reaction is panic, since "being

man" is largely dependent on sexual success. For the woman, the situation creates tremendous anxiety: If she attempts to reassure her partner, he may interpret it as "sympathy," which then confirms his feelings of inadequacy. But if, out of misguided consideration, she attempts to brush it off as unimportant, he's apt to interpret this as contempt.

The correct answer is: (C)

If we weren't so work-oriented, we'd focus more on the enjoyment of love-making and less on the orgasm. Instead, we *quantify* sex ("We made love three times today" much as we say, "I played nine holes of golf") and diminish the *quality*. When we stop viewing sex as a performance with a score card, we can relax and enjoy it as an experience in intimacy, with no goal but the giving and receiving of mutual pleasure.

"Sexual Communication"

The correct answer is: (C)

Asking for what we want does not *ensure* our getting it—after all, a request is not the same as a demand—but the odds of our getting it go way up, especially if we send a clear message. Being "too embarrassed to ask" starts a circular process in which *not asking* leads to *not getting* and then to *being mad* at one's partner for not knowing! And wanting things to happen spontaneously is like searching for a new address in a strange city without a map, hoping to suddenly hit upon it. It *could* happen—but don't count on it.

The correct answers are: (A) and (B)

Assuming is a dangerous path. A far safer route is

to discover exactly what is pleasing, either by asking specifically or by exploring physically (as long as the sensations are then verified by direct questions such as: "Are you telling me that you want *more* of what I'm doing?").

3. *The correct answer is:* (*A*)

For two people to enjoy sex maximally, both must be able to state what they want, hear one another, and, if possible, accede to the other's request. (However, when a person desires something that his/her partner finds objectionable but does anyway out of fear of disapproval, the aversion is only reinforced.) One way to handle this is for each one to share with the other: Things I like, Things I Don't Like, and Things I'm Willing to Try—At Least Once.

For some people, sex=intercourse=missionary position, *despite* evidence which suggests that the missionary position is the *least* likely to satisfy the woman and the *most* likely to result in premature ejaculation for the man.

4. *The correct answer is:* (*C*)

Girls learn to talk at a much earlier age than boys, and never lose that advantage! In sex as well as in other areas, verbalizing seems to be easier for women, so for men who find it difficult or distracting, a good substitute is "soft lights and sweet music," especially music that both partners find erotic, or at least pleasurable.

5. *The correct answer is:* (*B*)

Being surprised *can* be exciting, but it can also prove disappointing. For those who feel that "asking takes the romance out of it," perhaps the best response is that, while sex is "perfectly natural," it is seldom "naturally perfect"!

6. *The correct answer is:* (*C*)

No one can ever know for sure exactly what someone else wants at that particular moment, so, without guidelines, we are all flying blind. This idea of only telling the partner when it's pleasing is especially prevalent for women (due to their conditioning regarding the "delicate male ego"). Add to that the man's "logical" thinking that "If I were doing something *wrong*, she'd tell me . . . ." and the stage is set for sexual disaster!

7. and 8. *The correct answers are* (B) *in both.*

One of the most frequently heard complaints of men has to do with the lack of response on the part of their partners. Women, on the other hand, often express the fear that their partners will think them "unfeminine" and, besides after fifteen or twenty years of repressing sexual feelings, women don't suddenly feel free enough to "let go" with murmurs, sounds, etc.

"Touching"

---

1. *The correct answer is:* (C)

The desire to be held, embraced, and fondled is almost unanimously expressed by women who complain over and over that their partners never caress them except when they're in bed. The interpret this as: "He's only interested in *sex* . . . not in *me!*" Such men, however, are actually not interested in sex—they are interested only in releasing tension.

2. *The correct answer is:* (D)

How important is touching? Well, two American anthropologists working in Japan noted the coincidence of those age periods when *sleeping alone* was most likely to occur with the age periods when *suicide* was most likely to occur. Noting that the rates for both types of behavior were highest in adolescence and again in old age, they concluded that it might be that sleeping alone (for people in these two age spans) contributes to a sense of isolation and alienation. An individual throughout the rest of his life seems to derive a sense of being a meaningful person from sleeping physically close to another person.

3. *The correct answer is:* (*A*)

Women who first experience Masters and Johnson's "Sensate Focus" exercises tend to be almost deliriously happy. "This is what I've been asking for all my life!" is a typical response. The idea of a lover caring enough to explore and find her most responsive areas is as important as the touch of his hands, lips, etc. As for men, they are often surprised to discover that other areas of their bodies are erogenous besides the genital area. Once over the initial surprise, however, they tend to react as positively as their partners.

4. *The correct answer is:* (*D*)

For women as well as men, childhood taboos regarding the body often reassert themselves when it comes to using the lips or the tongue over specific areas.

5. *The correct answer is:* (*C*)

Not only is each woman different from every other woman, but each woman is different on Monday from what she may have wanted on Sunday. And the same is true for men, although perhaps to a lesser degree. Under these circumstances, how is one to know what his/her partner desires unless he is shown, led, guided, etc.? And since we are constantly changing, "remembering" is not the key, but rather "discovering anew."

6. *The correct answer is:* (*A*)

In too many people's minds, "massage" is associated with being kneaded, pounded, and rubbed—often an impersonal, indifferent, and sometimes painful experience. Also in the United States today, some "massage parlors" now operate as fronts for houses of prostitution . . . yet this tells us something about the erotic link between massage and sex. "Massage" in this connotation refers to the continuous firm but gentle rhythmic communication with and for another person.

"Fragrances"

---

1. *The correct answer is:* (*B*)

When our sense of smell is at work, we are usually aware of different odors, and when we are really "tuned in" to another we notice new scents, much as we notice a new hairstyle or new clothing.

2. *The correct answer is:* (*A*)

Naming a partner's fragrances is less important than *noticing* them and remarking about them. Here, too, the emphasis is on the idea of being *aware of* and *responsive* to another human being, which is the essence of loving.

3. *The correct answer is:* (*A*)

Because we have developed the custom of daily showers, the scent of a "squeaky-clean" body is pleasurable. However, what is *erotic* is individual taste and a person may *like* a clean body odor but be *excited* by certain scents. (Try shopping *together* for new fragrances. That, too, can be an adventure.)

4. *The correct answers are both* (*A*) *and* (*B*)

People who perspire at work or play tend to find the odor of perspiration more pleasant than those who lead more sedentary lives.

5. *The correct answer is:* (*A*)

Persons who are free to enjoy their bodies would be most likely to choose (A), "titillating," as their answer. Persons least in touch with their bodies, or least accepting of them, would tend to choose (C), "definitely unpleasant." However, again, it depends on the individuals.

6. *The correct answers are: (A) and (B)*

(A) and (B) would be the preferred answers because touching, caressing, and fondling are all a part of the love play that makes sex so enjoyable. (Try it, you'll like it!)

7. *The correct answer is: (A)*

Not only does bathing together create a feeling of caring and togetherness, it also symbolizes, "I care enough about you to devote time *to* you." It's a *literal showering* of attention.

"Disrobing"

---

1. *The correct answer is: (A)*

Undressing each other can be sensual as well as an indication of caring. Undressing in private, watching the other undress, and undressing efficiently are all somewhat passive and indicate a certain degree of noninvolvement with one's partner.

2. *The correct answer is: (C)*

Soft lights can be stimulating, adding a sense of mystery and romance to the scene. Instead of "feeling embarrassed," partners can plan together to create an erotic environment.

3. *The correct answer is: (C)*

Visual experience is just taking advantage of one more sense in mutual enjoyment. Regardless of what you may look like in your own eyes, if your partner didn't find you exciting, he/she wouldn't be there!

HOW DO YOU SCORE THIS TEST?

You don't. No one passes, no one fails. But if you got more than six or seven wrong, or if you took this test with your partner and your answers didn't parallel each other's 85 per cent of the time, your sexual quotient needs work. At least you can begin talking about it.

And that's the purpose of our test. Perhaps some of you will gain a better understanding of sex—a new awareness that it is the deepest form of expression of love, intimacy, and caring.

Also, it can be a lot of fun!

THE LAST WORD
ON LOVE, SEX, AND MARRIAGE?"

"DOESN'T IT TAKE A LONG TIME
TO LEARN ABOUT LOVE, SEX, AND MARRIAGE?"

Well, you're living while you're learning, and I think some people forget that and just hold their breath until they have learned everything. You can't do that. You have to start living now. Now is now. And life takes a long time, too.

"ISN'T LIFE OVER BEFORE YOU LEARN
HOW TO LIVE IT?"

"I don't think so. I'm getting older and time seems to be going faster. But, at the same time, I'm enjoying each day. Just get whatever you can get for now. Don't live in the past or in the future.

Mildred Newman
New York, New York

the national sampling

SAMPLING

A sample of twenty cities was selected as interview sites which represent relevant aspect of the nation as a whole. These cities were selected in the following fashion.

First, the country was broken into four geographic regions:

Far West	(California, Washington, Idaho, Colorado, and New Mexico)
Midwest	(Texas, Missouri, Nebraska, and Iowa)
South	(Florida, Georgia, North Carolina, and Maryland)
North/Northeast	(Illinois, Michigan, Ohio, New York, Massachusetts, and Maine)

Next, the nation's top three hundred metropolitan markets were identified. These markets were divided into three groups representing large, medium, and small communities. Representative cities of each size were then selected within each geographic area.

Approximately fifty interviews were conducted in each city during the weekend of November 18 and 19, 1977, at intercept locations. A weekend was chosen so that working men and women would be included in the sample. All interviews were completed in a forty-eight-hour period to ensure comparability of responses.

An intercept technique was used in the actual selection of respondents. In each city, two locations (one central, one suburban) were utilized, and the interviewers were assigned to specific shopping-center locations to ensure access to the largest number of possible respondents.

Extensive instructions were given the interviewers for administering the questionnaire to persons over the age of eighteen, males and females, and both single and married individuals. (See discussion of individual variables below.) In order to minimize coding errors, respondents verbally reported responses to the interviewer, who then marked the response on the questionnaire form. (In pretesting the questionnaire, it was found that the respondent needed minimal guidance from the interviewer.) Respondents were only given advice if the question referred to "your mate" and the respondent was single; in such cases interviewers encouraged the respondent to answer as if he or she were married. However, if the respondent felt he or she absolutely could not answer, the interviewer was to skip that particular question and continue with the rest of the questionnaire. Because of the relatively short length of the interview (approximately twelve minutes), respondent interest remained high.

THE TEST

The test appeared to be a success in terms of over-all performance. It offered a challenge and stimulus to many without being too demanding. On the average, people missed about one question in four (the average of correct responses for all subjects was 74 per cent). Some individuals did better than others, however. Five respondents (.5 per cent of the sample) answered all questions correctly, while one person received a score of 8 correct out of 31 questions. Looking at the different sections, we see that respondents were least aware of the issues presented in the LOVE and ROLES sections, averaging only 3.2 correct out of a possible 5. On the other hand, respondents did very well on the TRUST section, with an average of 4.1 correct out of a possible 5.

Within sections, we see that some specific items were more difficult than others. One item was answered correctly only about 16 per cent of the time: ROLES 2, "People are often less satisfied with their marriages if they have children." On the other hand, 93 per cent of the respondents gave the correct answer of FEELINGS 3, "Crying is a sign of weakness." (See Table 1 for a summary of the percent of respondents with the correct answer for these and other questions.)

MALE/FEMALE

Quotas were established for the selection of respondents to yield approximately equal numbers of males and females. These parameters were achieved with considerable accuracy in the actual sample with 510 (49.5 per cent) female respondents and 520 (50.5 per cent) male respondents.

The differences between male and female respondents are of some interest. On the average, women were correct in their responses 4.5 per cent more often than men. In their over-all scores on the average, women answered 75.5 per cent of the questions correctly answered by men. While not a great absolute difference between average scores, it should be noted that women with a high degree of consistency gave *more* correct answers than men. In 27 out of the 31 questions, women more often answered correctly. Thus, it would appear that women are more sensitive to the issue of relationships to the extent that they are able to provide the socially acceptable responses required for the test.

Perhaps the most noticeable single item differentiating women's and men's responses was concerned with child care and the mother's labor force status (ROLES 4). The item, calling for a true or false response, asserted: "If a wife works, the children will have more problems than if she stays at home." While the majority of people disagreed with this statement, men did so in only 55.6 per cent of the cases while 70.7 per cent of the women disagreed. Evidently more men than women still feel that the traditional place of the woman in the home is important at least for the proper care and supervision of children. Noticeable disagreement was also evident regarding the proper role of men versus women in making major decisions within a relationship. ROLES 5 stated, "It's up to the man to primarily make the basic decisions in a relationship." Again, the majority of the respondents disagreed, but males (67.2 per cent) less frequently than females (79.1 per cent). Apparently more men (12 per cent) than women in our sample see the male as the principal decision-maker.

MARITAL STATUS

It should be noted that the figures reported here represent a collapsing of categories from the original data collected, in which respondents indicated their marital status as either (1) married, (2) single, (3) divorced, (4) widowed, (5) separated, or (6) living together. These categories have been reduced to "married" and "single" by combining persons indicating their marital status as "living together" with the married group and all others within the "single" category. In grouping the categories together in this fashion, *current* marital status may be used as a rough indicator of whether the respondent had a current intimate partner he or she could refer to in answering the test questions.

The methodological difficulties which might otherwise be attendant to such a collapsing of categories are mitigated, at least in part, by the small numbers of persons involved: divorced (80), widowed (20), separated (23), and living together (50). In addition, the prior analysis in which each category of marital status was analyzed independently revealed little difference between the married and single groups. This relationship persists after the data are recoded. Differences are not, however, totally absent.

One interesting finding obscured by the collapsing of categories is that approximately 5 per cent of the sample (50 respondents) indicated their marital status as "living together." This figure may disproportionately reflect the attitudes of the younger age groupings of which the sample is in large part comprised. Nonetheless, it does indicate the form that relationships between these young persons are taking.

A few notable differences between the two marital groups appeared in the test. "Married" persons felt that "sexual fantasies or daydreams . . . make a love relationship more exciting" more often (82.6 per cent) than "single" people (74.9 per cent). In addition, the marrieds felt embarrassed giving or receiving affection (FEELINGS 4) less often (45.7 per cent) than single people (54.3 per cent). Perhaps the intimacy of marriage provides opportunities for learning how to give and receive affection not present in the singles' world. As embarrassment about personal affection wanes for married people, so evidently do their restrictions about sexual fantasy and daydreams, and these are seen as contributing to the quality of their love relationship.

With this greater libidinal freedom and openness to give and receive affection comes another change in relationships. Apparently a marital relationship between persons builds trust at least with regard to their behavior in public places with others. TRUST 3 states: "At a party, if an attractive person of the oppostie sex pays a lot of attention to my mate, I would . . ." Of the "married" respondents, 70.1 per cent said they would "have confidence in my mate," while only 57.5 per cent of the "single" individuals answered similarly. Other questions did not produce such marked differences.

AGE

Quotas were structured so that there were more respondents in the eighteen–thirty-five-year-old range than in other age groups. This is the age at which persons are most likely to be married for the first time (median age for first marriage is approximately twenty-four years for males and twenty-one years for females). In addition, many individuals in this age range may be experiencing the difficulties of divorce and the initiation of new relationships, since many divorces occur after the first few years of marriage.

Persons under eighteen years of age were excluded since, prior to that age, males, females, or both are prohibited in many jurisdictions from marrying without parental consent or other special procedures. The sample, therefore, was designed to obtain 75 per cent of the respondents in the critical eighteen—thirty-five-year-old group and 50 per cent in the eighteen–twenty-nine category. These goals were achieved with notable success. In the actual age distribution of respondents, 54 per cent were between eighteen and twenty-nine years of age and approximately 74 per cent were between eighteen and thirty-five. Thus, the sample is not representative of the United States population as a whole, but emphasizes the age groups most likely to be initiating an ongoing intimate relationship and dealing with the problems associated with such a relationship. For the purposes of reporting, the age groups are referred to as "under 30" and "over 30," comprising 54.1 per cent and 45.9 per cent of the total sample respectively.

Some noticeable disagreement appeared between the "under 30" and "over 30" groups' views of the effect fighting has on a relationship. FIGHTING 5 asserts: "Fighting can actually lead to a better relationship." Almost 70 per cent of the "under 30" group agreed with this statement while less than 60 per cent of the "over 30" group agreed. There was a lack of agreement between the two age groups on another point. On TRUST 3 ("At a party, if an attractive person of the opposite sex pays a lot of attention to my mate, I would . . ."), we observe that approximately 60 per cent of the "under 30" group would "have confidence in [their] mate," while almost 70 per cent of the "over 30" group expressed this confidence. This latter difference may result from the greater length of time relationships have lasted between members of the "over 30" group, giving them experience upon which to base their trust. The "under 30" group undoubtedly contains a higher proportion of unmarried people, who, as we noted above, are less trusting in such a situation.

GEOGRAPHIC REGION

While the other variables used in looking at people's responses (sex, age, marital status) produced only a few differences, there appear to be numerous differences in the responses of persons from different regions of the country. The most noticeable of these discrepancies lies between people in the Midwest and those in other parts of the country. Midwesterners were consistently at odds with the "right" answers to questions, scoring lower than people from other regions in all categories.

Over-all, the best performance was put in by respondents from the Far West, who got approximately 77 per cent of all questions correct, followed by the North/Northeast and South, with approximately 73 per cent correct, and finally the Midwest, with 69 per cent answered correctly.

LOVE 2 states, "True love is something that always lasts a lifetime." While almost 70 per cent of the westerners scored this correctly as a false statement, only 50 per cent

of the midwesterners said it was false. In the section of
SEX, Question 6 reads, "The most common difficulty in a
loving relationship is . . ." In the West about 74 per cent
answered correctly by choosing "communication problems." In the Midwest only about 61 per cent favored this
response, with almost one third of them selecting "money
problems." In the section of ROLES, Question 5 indicated
that men are the ones who primarily make decisions in a
relationship. Seventy-nine per cent of the North/northeast-
erners identified this as false, while only 60 per cent of the
midwesterners scored it a false statement. Regarding
fighting, only 27 per cent of the westerners felt that "people usually argue about what really bothers them"
(FIGHTING 1), while more than 54 per cent of the
midwestern repondents felt this was the case. FEEL-
INGS 3 asserts that "crying is a sign of weakness." While
a very small number of respondents throughout the nation
agreed with this statement, those that did came disproportionately from the Midwest, with 17.5 per cent in agreement, compared with only 5.2 per cent from the West.
Finally, in TRUST 3 ("At a party, if an attractive person of the opposite sex pays a lot of attention to my mate,
I would . . ."), only about 55 per cent of the midwesterners would "have confidence in [their] mate[s]," while
almost 70 per cent of the western respondents expressed
such confidence.

The midwesterners, in contrast to people from other
parts of the country, convey an image of one who believes
more in a romantic ideal ("one love forever") than the
realities of actual relations with a mate. They are propor-
tionally more concerned with materialistic rather than
communication difficulties in a relationship, an oversight
reflected in their belief that people usually argue about important matters. They believe in male supremacy, at least
in decision-making, and, in complementary fashion, believe
that crying, a traditional female behavior, is a sign of
weakness. In addition, they have less trust in their mates
than others—at least when it involves their partners and a
person of the opposite sex. In sum, the Midwest appears to
reflect a more traditional view of the relationship between

partners than other areas of the nation and a marked difference between the acceptable and expected behaviors of males and females.

OUTSTANDING ITEMS

Perhaps the most interesting item on the test ROLES 2, "People are often less satisfied with their marriages if they have children." Only 16 per cent of all respondents recognized this statement as a correct reflection of research findings on marital satisfaction. Apparently the widespread popular belief in the joys of parenthood obscured respondents' evaluation of their own or others' actual experience as parents and the effects of parenthood on the husband-wife relationship in determining their answers. They were perhaps trying to provide what they considered the socially acceptable (if not a personally accurate) answer to the question. After all, denial of motherhood as a valued state puts one perilously close to heresy, for can a rejection of God, Country, and Apple Pie be far behind? The consistency with which the false response was selected suggests a universal rather than a demographic subgroup misconception.

Another similarly atypical item which might be worthy of comment is LOVE 1: "Jealousy is natural if you really love your mate." Only 46 per cent of the respondents agreed with the experts that this is a false statement and there was also some variation among the demographic subgroupings. Jealousy was considered natural more often by males, single persons, those under thirty, and people from the North/Northeast.

Another item with considerable ability to discriminate among the various demographic subgroupings in the test was TRUST 3 (the "at a party" question we've examined previously). As we mentioned, considerable differences were observed in the responses to this question between males and females (7.4 per cent), those under thirty and over thirty (10 per cent difference), and between those in the Far West and those in the Midwest (14 per cent difference). Males, those under thirty, and Midwesterners are less likely to be totally trusting of their mates in the circumstance described.

Table I—Explanation

Table 1 is intended as a quick summary of people's answers to all items on the questionnaire, divided into the various demographic subgroups identified in the study. *All of the numbers in Part A of Table 1 represent the PER CENT OF RESPONDENTS correctly answering that question.*

In the left column is each question as asked on the test, followed by abbreviation of the right answer. In the next column is the section name and number of the question. We note, for example, that the first question on the table reads, "Jealousy is natural if you really love your mate. (F)" followed by LOVE 1. Thus, this is the first question in the LOVE section and the correct answer is "False."

To the right of the question is a series of numbers indicating the per cent of the sample who gave the correct answer for each question in each of the demographic groupings indicated along the top of the page. For example, following LOVE 1, we see the numbers 53.6, 40.5, and 49.5 in a row to the right beneath the headings, "Far West," "Midwest," and "South." Therefore, we know that 53.6 per cent of the respondents in the Far West correctly answered the LOVE 1 question, "Jealousy is natural if you really love your mate," by marking it "False." Similarly, 40.5 per cent of the midwestern respondents and 49.5 per cent of the southern participants got the right answer.

The far right column is labeled "All Respondents" and provides the per cent of persons in the sample answering each question correctly. We can see, therefore, that 45.8 per cent of *all* respondents got question LOVE 1 right.

By finding the intersection of any question number and any demographic grouping, the per cent of people giving the correct answer for that question in any particular demograhic group can be easily determined. For example, if we were interested in the responses of males and females to the question "If a wife works, the children will have more problems than if she stays home," we would find the question in the left column with the correct answer indicated as (F), False. We note that this is ROLES 4 (the fourth question in the ROLES section of the test). Looking at the top of the page, we locate the columns labeled "Male" and "Female" and follow them down to the intersection with the ROLES 4 row. There we see that 55.6 per cent of the male respondents and 70.7 per cent of the female respondents answered this question correctly.

Part B of Table I contains percentages which have been computed from the individual responses in Part A. The headings labeled "LOVE," "SEX," "ROLES," "FIGHTING," "FEELINGS," "TRUST," and "OVER-ALL" represent the sample's performance on a *given section* of the test and their performance on the test as a *whole. All the numbers in this section represent PER CENT OF QUESTIONS, ON THE AVERAGE, that the sample answered correctly.*

Similarities or difference in the average per cent of correct answers for each section or for the test as a whole for various demographic subgroupings can be found in this part of the table. For example, finding the intersection of the "ROLES" column and the Male and Female columns, we see that male respondents, on the average, got about 63 per cent of all questions in the ROLES section correct, while female respondents, on the average, correctly answered 70 per cent of those questions.

Beneath the computed variables in Part B of Table I is another block of figures labeled "Part C—Average Frequency of Correct Responses by Section."

As the title suggests, this section of the table indicates *how many questions*, on the average, were answered correctly in each section of the test, computed in the same fashion as described above, but *not* converted to percentages.

One final note: At the top of the table with each of the demographic subgroup headings is a number enclosed in parentheses. This figure indicates the number of respondents who fell into that subgroup. For example, the heading "Single" includes "(N=461)," which signifies that there were 461 respondents in the sample whose marital status was single.

TABLE I - PART A: PER CENT CORRECT

Section/ Question	Jealousy is natural if you really love your mate. (F)	True love is something that always lasts a lifetime. (F)	Taking my side—no matter what—shows my partner loves me. (F)	Just because two people break up doesn't mean they never loved each other. (T)	If people really love each other, they don't have to say it. (F)
	LOVE 1	LOVE 2	LOVE 3	LOVE 4	LOVE 5
All Respondents (N=1,032)	45.8	59.1	82.3	77.6	52.7
Over 30 (N=473)	49.8	60.0	82.9	75.5	50.0
Under 30 (N=557)	42.3	58.3	81.7	79.4	55.0
Single (N=461)	41.2	61.7	81.3	77.0	50.4
Married (N=565)	49.2	57.0	83.0	78.2	54.6
Female (N=510)	49.4	57.2	82.9	78.4	54.1
Male (N=520)	42.1	60.8	81.5	76.7	51.2
North/Northeast (N=311)	39.0	53.4	79.4	73.3	45.5
South (N=210)	49.5	60.5	83.7	76.2	56.9
Midwest (N=200)	40.5	50.0	78.5	78.5	52.0
Far West (N=311)	53.6	69.7	86.5	82.0	57.6

	SEX										
Hugging and cuddling are: important and different from making love. (B)	SEX 1	91.1	85.5	89.0	86.5	86.7	89.9	87.0	89.8	91.2	84.5	88.2
Sexual fantasies, or daydreams: make a love relationship more exciting. (A)	SEX 2	81.1	78.7	79.6	78.5	77.1	81.1	82.6	74.9	79.3	78.8	79.1
The main responsibility for birth control should be with: both mates together. (C)	SEX 3	84.9	82.0	86.7	84.9	82.5	87.1	85.3	83.7	85.3	83.9	84.7
When making love: you have to tell your mate what is pleasing. (B)	SEX 4	82.6	70.8	79.8	80.2	79.7	78.3	79.3	78.7	78.4	79.8	79.0
As the years pass, I expect that my love life with my partner will: improve. (C)	SEX 5	88.1	82.7	88.0	85.8	83.7	89.1	89.5	82.3	87.6	84.7	86.3
The most common difficulty in a loving relationship is: communication problems. (B)	SEX 6	73.7	61.3	65.2	67.0	64.9	70.5	66.1	69.3	68.7	66.1	67.5

TABLE I - PART A: PER CENT CORRECT (cont.)

Section/Question	Question	All Respondents (N=1,032)	Over 30 (N=473)	Under 30 (N=557)	Single (N=461)	Married (N=565)	Female (N=510)	Male (N=520)	North/Northeast (N=311)	South (N=210)	Midwest (N=200)	Far West (N=311)
ROLES 1	A woman who works can't be as good a mate as one who doesn't. (F)	85.4	83.9	86.5	85.2	85.6	87.6	83.0	86.8	86.2	81.0	86.1
ROLES 2	People are often less satisfied with their marriages if they have children. (T)	15.9	17.6	14.5	16.3	15.6	14.3	17.3	14.8	17.6	14.0	17.1
ROLES 3	Men don't like women to take the lead in love-making. (F)	81.2	82.4	80.3	77.3	84.4	82.8	79.6	78.1	84.3	75.5	86.0
ROLES 4	If a wife works, the children will have more problems than if she stays home. (F)	62.9	60.7	64.9	63.0	63.1	70.7	55.6	64.2	68.1	56.0	62.7
ROLES 5	It's up to the man to primarily make the basic decisions in a relationship. (F)											

People usually argue about what really bothers them. (F)

The longer you fight, the more likely you are to reach a permanent solution. (F)

It's possible to have two winners in an argument. (T)

It's best just to argue about one problem at a time and not bring up the past. (T)

Fighting can actually lead to a better relationship. (T)

FIGHTING 1	72.6	45.7	65.2	58.8	60.9	62.7	63.8	59.9	57.9	66.5	61.7
FIGHTING 2	88.1	79.5	83.8	83.3	81.0	87.3	86.9	80.5	81.1	87.5	84.1
FIGHTING 3	85.1	73.0	79.5	81.7	80.5	81.1	81.7	79.1	82.9	77.8	80.6
FIGHTING 4	87.7	87.9	80.0	89.7	83.8	89.8	88.3	85.0	84.7	89.4	86.8
FIGHTING 5	65.1	65.8	63.2	65.7	64.3	65.9	63.7	66.9	69.9	59.4	65.0

TABLE I - PART A: PER CENT CORRECT (cont.)

Section/Question	All Respondents (N=1,032)	Over 30 (N=473)	Under 30 (N=557)	Single (N=461)	Married (N=565)	Female (N=510)	Male (N=520)	North/Northeast (N=311)	South (N=210)	Midwest (N=200)	Far West (N=311)
FEELINGS 1 There is no way to know for sure what your mate feels unless they tell you. (F)	58.7	57.0	60.3	58.7	58.7	60.5	57.1	64.0	55.2	54.8	58.3
FEELINGS 2 If people have any pride at all, they're not going to say, "I'm sorry." (F)	93.2	92.4	94.0	93.2	93.4	93.5	92.9	91.6	93.8	90.0	96.4
FEELINGS 3 Crying is a sign of weakness. (F)	90.5	92.4	88.8	89.3	91.3	93.5	87.5	91.0	91.0	82.5	94.8
FEELINGS 4 I often feel embarrassed giving or receiving affection. (F)	75.1	78.9	71.9	70.0	79.5	78.4	71.9	75.9	75.2	76.5	73.2
FEELINGS 5 I would rather say, "I don't want to tell you," than to lie. (T)	80.1	77.5	82.2	83.9	76.9	83.8	76.3	81.9	73.7	77.5	84.1

Item	TRUST											
The partners who have the most freedom in their relationship are those: who respect the rights, the freedom and privacy of their partner. (B)	TRUST 1	92.6	88.9	89.0	88.4	87.4	92.3	91.1	88.5	91.0	88.8	89.9
If two people trust each other, it's okay to: discuss what kind of privacy they want. (C)	TRUST 2	95.4	85.5	87.6	87.4	87.9	91.1	87.4	92.2	91.7	86.8	89.5
At a party, if an attractive person of the opposite sex pays a lot of attention to my mate, I would: have confidence in my mate. (A)	TRUST 3	69.3	55.3	60.3	68.5	66.3	62.7	70.1	57.5	59.9	69.9	64.5
If I discovered my mate had an affair with someone else, I would: talk about it and work things out. (C)	TRUST 4	82.9	76.1	78.9	78.4	76.4	82.6	80.5	78.0	79.1	80.0	79.4
If my mate has a hobby that I don't care for, it is best: for each of us to give in a little. (C)	TRUST 5	91.1	85.9	87.6	85.9	87.2	88.5	86.9	88.9	88.2	87.4	87.8

TABLE I - PART B: AVERAGE PER CENT CORRECT PER TEST SECTION

TEST SECTION	Number of Questions Per Section	Far West (N=311)	Midwest (N=200)	South (N=210)	North/Northeast (N=311)	Male (N=520)	Female (N=510)	Married (N=565)	Single (N=461)	Under 30 (N=557)	Over 30 (N=473)	All Respondents (N=1,032)
"LOVE"	5	70.0	60.0	64.0	58.0	62.0	64.0	64.0	62.0	64.0	64.0	64.0
"SEX"	6	78.0	71.8	74.2	74.4	73.3	80.0	76.7	75.0	76.7	75.0	76.6
"ROLES"	5	64.0	58.0	66.0	64.0	60.0	66.0	64.0	62.0	64.0	64.0	64.0
"FIGHTING"	5	80.0	70.0	74.0	76.0	74.0	78.0	76.0	74.0	76.0	76.0	76.0
"FEELINGS"	5	82.0	76.0	78.0	80.0	78.0	82.0	80.0	80.0	80.0	80.0	80.0
"TRUST"	5	86.0	78.0	80.6	82.0	82.0	84.0	84.0	82.0	82.0	82.0	82.0
"OVER-ALL"	31	76.8	69.0	72.6	72.6	71.0	75.5	74.2	72.3	73.2	73.5	73.8

TABLE I - PART C: AVERAGE FREQUENCY OF CORRECT RESPONSES BY SECTION

TEST SECTION	All Respondents (N=1,032)	Over 30 (N=473)	Under 30 (N=557)	Single (N=461)	Married (N=565)	Female (N=510)	Male (N=520)	North/Northeast (N=311)	South (N=210)	Midwest (N=200)	Far West (N=311)	Number of Questions Per Section
"LOVE"	3.2	3.2	3.2	3.1	3.2	3.2	3.1	2.9	3.2	3.0	3.5	5
"SEX"	4.6	4.5	4.6	4.5	4.6	4.8	4.4	4.5	4.4	4.3	4.7	6
"ROLES"	3.2	3.2	3.2	3.1	3.2	3.3	3.0	3.2	3.3	2.9	3.2	5
"FIGHTING"	3.8	3.8	3.8	3.7	3.8	3.9	3.7	3.8	3.7	3.5	4.0	5
"FEELINGS"	4.0	4.0	4.0	4.0	4.0	4.1	3.9	4.0	3.9	3.8	4.1	5
"TRUST"	4.1	4.1	4.1	4.1	4.2	4.2	4.1	4.1	4.0	3.9	4.3	5
"OVER-ALL"	22.9	22.8	22.7	22.4	23.0	23.4	22.0	22.5	22.5	21.4	23.8	31

Table II—Explanation

Table II provides a brief overview of the responses of *all persons* in the sample *considered together*.

Each test question is listed in the order in which it appears throughout the book. Each question is proceeded by the section and question number, as in Table I (e.g., LOVE 1). This in turn is followed by the actual question and the possible responses. The per cent of all respondents answering in each response category is indicated and the correct answer marked with an asterisk. For example, on the first line, LOVE 1 refers to the first item in the love section. That actual question is: "Jealousy is natural if you really love your mate." We see that 54.3 per cent of all respondents indicated this statement was true, while 45.7 per cent correctly answered the statement "False." The remaining questions may be interpreted similarly.

TABLE II

FREQUENCY DISTRIBUTION
OF RESPONDENTS' ANSWERS (IN PER CENT)

LOVE 1
Jealousy is natural if you really love your mate.

54.3 True
* 45.7 False

LOVE 2
True love is something that always lasts a lifetime.

40.9 True
* 59.1 False

LOVE 3
Taking my side—no matter what—shows my partner loves me.

17.7 True
* 82.3 False

LOVE 4
Just because two people break up doesn't mean they never loved each other.

* 77.5 True
22.5 False

LOVE 5
If people really love each other, they don't have to say it.

47.3 True
* 52.7 False

SEX 1
Hugging and cuddling are:
    A) not important if people really love each other.   8.1
* B) important and different from making love.   88.2*
    C) only important before making love.   3.7

SEX 2
Sexual fantasies, or daydreams:

* A) make a love relationship more ex-
     citing.   79.1*
  B) show there is something missing in
     your relationship.   19.2
  C) lead to sex crimes.   1.7

SEX 3
The main responsibility for birth control
should be with:
  A) the woman.   13.4
  B) the man.   1.9
* C) both mates together.   84 7*

SEX 4
When making love:
  A) people naturally know what do do   17.6
* B) you having to tell your mate what is
        pleasing.   79.0*

SEX 5
As the years pass, I expect that my love life
with my partner will:
  A) fade away.   6.2
  B) become less satisfying.   7.4
* C) improve.   86.3*

SEX 6
The most common difficulty in a loving
relationship is:
  A) money problems.   28.9
* B) communication problems.   67.5*
  C) physical incompatibility.   3.5

ROLES 1
A woman who works can't be as good a   14.7 True
mate as one who doesn't   * 85.3 False

ROLES 2
People are often less satisfied with their * 15.9 True
marriages if they have children.   84.1 False

ROLES 3
Men don't like women to take the lead in love-making.

18.8 True
* 81.2 False

ROLES 4
If a wife works, the children will have more problems than if she stays at home.

37.1 True
* 62.9 False

ROLES 5
It's up to the man to primarily make the basic decisions in a relationship.

26.9 True
* 73.1 False

FIGHTING 1
People usually argue about what really bothers them.

38.3 True
* 61.7 False

FIGHTING 2
The longer you fight, the more likely you are to reach a permanent solution.

15.9 True
* 84.1 False

FIGHTING 3
It's possible to have two winners in an argument.

* 80.6 True
19.4 False

FIGHTING 4
It's best just to argue about one problem at a time and not bring up the past.

* 86.8 True
13.2 False

FIGHTING 5
Fighting can actually lead to a better relationship.

* 65.0 True
35.0 False

FEELINGS 1
There is no way to know for sure what your mate feels unless they tell you.

* 58.7 True
41.3 False

FEELINGS 2
If people have any pride at all, they're not going to say, "I'm sorry."

6.8 True
* 93.2 False

FEELINGS 3
Crying is a sign of weakness.

9.5 True
* 90.5 False

FEELINGS 4

I often feel embarrassed giving or receiving affection.

24.9 True
* 75.1 False

FEELINGS 5

I would rather say, "I don't want to tell you," than to lie.

* 80.1 True
19.9 False

TRUST 1

The partners who have the most freedom in their relationship are those:

   A) who live together without being married.   5.6

* B) who respect the rights, the freedom and privacy, of their partner.   89.9*

   C) who are financially successful.   4.5

TRUST 2

If two people trust each other, it's okay to:

   A) open each other's mail.   8.1

   B) listen in on the phone, but not open the other's mail.   2.4

* C) discuss what kind of privacy they want.   89.5*

TRUST 3

At a party, if an attractive person of the opposite sex pays a lot of attention to my mate, I would:

* A) have confidence in my mate.   64.5*

   B) try to attract someone else, too.   6.2

   C) try to conceal my feelings.   29.3

TRUST 4

If I discovered my mate had an affair with someone else, I would:

   A) know my mate didn't love me any more.   13.4

   B) have an affair myself.   7.2

* C) talk about it and work things out.   79.4*

TRUST 5

If my mate has a hobby that I don't care
for, it is best:

    A) to do it, too, even if I don't like it.   5.7

    B) for my mate to do something else
        we can both enjoy.   6.5

*   C) for each of us to give in a little.   87.8*